The

HIP HOP
PRAYER BOOK

HipHopEMass in the News

"Popular Christian music styles have always paralleled the sound of secular hits, from grunge to techno. Now hip-hop is finding its way into the liturgies of traditional churches. [Reverend] Holder developed 'The Hip Hop Prayer Book,' inspired by the Book of Common Prayer, which he wrote with help from dozens of rappers, musicians and poets. Proponents argue that using vernacular language in services is a way to draw young people to church. Everyone's down with that." —*Newsweek*

"After one early HipHopEMass—the experiment began with a string of Friday night services in the summer of 2004—an elated little girl looked Poppa T in the eye and gave him a confidence boost: 'Jesus is so real to have a hip-hop mass,' she gushed."
—*The Village Voice*

"At Saturday's [hip hop Mass] of about 200 young people and church leaders, Father Holder preached that a church that does not have the street at its altar and its altar in the street cannot last long. He discussed how to start a hip-hop Mass at local congregations: be sure to listen to all rap songs first, to screen out any cursing, misogyny or homophobia; and let the children lead."
—*New York Times*

"[The HipHopEMass] artists and adherents find in hip-hop's outlaw reputation a challenge to Christian orthodoxy and a prophetic call to embrace modern society's version of the biblical outcasts whose company, they'll tell you, Jesus preferred. Thugs and gangsters as well as gays and lesbians are specifically included. And if none of the artists in this camp are currently found on the Christian rap charts, they're confident that, eventually, inclusion will not only sell but save,"—*Los Angeles Times*

"Holder is among the new leaders to emerge in the fast-growing, underground movement of holy hip-hop, a melding of religion, primarily Christianity, with the energy, lingo, dress and dance moves of the culture. The approach, created to attract young people and hip-hop fans, has produced a number of fledgling churches across the country, several traveling rap ministries, numerous Christian rap artists, a couple of awards shows and plenty of Wrath of God-like discussion from Long Island to the Bay Area."—*Newsday*

"Over the last three years, Poppa T has taken his eMass around the country (to over 25,000 congregants, according to his estimates) and has completed a CD ('And the Word Was Hip-Hop') as well as published a beautiful Hip Hop Prayer book that puts a new spin on ancient words."—*Black Voices*

"Hip hop and church probably seem like oil and water to most of you. Both can be great on their own, but they just don't mix together well. But don't tell 'Poppa T' that. Also known as Episcopal priest Timothy Holder, he's held a very popular hip hop Mass for the last two years."—ABCNews.com

"HipHopEMass, the syncopated lively ministry born on the streets of the Bronx, New York, has not skipped a beat since moving to the shores of New Jersey's Atlantic City." —*Episcopal Life Online*

"[Reverend] Holder is among a growing number of religious leaders to use holy hip-hop to reach younger generations, melding religion with the language, dress and dance moves of the culture that was born on the streets of the Bronx about 30 years ago." —*Reuters*

"Hip-HopEMass offers rich variety..." —*Sojourners Magazine*

Recipient of the Blessed are the Peacemakers Award from the World Council of Churches.

I am about to do a new thing; now it springs forth, do you not perceive it?

The

HIP HOP

PRAYER BOOK

EDITED BY
The Reverend Timothy Holder

THE REMIX

Seabury Books
NEW YORK

HIPHOPEMASS.ORG

Book design by Stefan Killen Design, NY

Seabury Press
445 Fifth Avenue
New York, NY 10016

ISBN 978-1-59627-090-9

Contents

Backup

Remix and New Birth

With thanks to The Introduction, Remix and Rebirth
THE HIP HOP PRAYER BOOK (2006)

"Poppa T"
The Reverend Timothy Holder
Rector, Historic Church of the Ascension
Founding Priest and Pastor, HipHopEMass
Atlantic City, New Jersey

Then Jesus, filled with the power of the Spirit, returned to Galilee...
When he came to Nazareth, where he had been brought up, he went
to the synagogue on the sabbath day, as was his custom. He stood
up to read, and the scroll of the prophet Isaiah was given to him.
He unrolled the scroll and found the place where it was written:

> "The Spirit of the Lord is
>   upon me,
> because he has anointed me
>   to bring good news to the
>   poor.
> He has sent me to proclaim
>   release to the captives
>   and recovery of sight to the
>   blind,
>   to let the oppressed go free,
> to proclaim the year of the Lord's
>   favor."

And he rolled up the scroll, gave it back to the attendant, and sat
down. The eyes of all in the synagogue were fixed on him. Then he

began to say to them, "Today this scripture has been fulfilled in your hearing." — **Luke 4:14-21**

"I am about to do a new thing; now it springs forth, do you not perceive it?," Isaiah shouts out in Isaiah 43:19. The 'new thing' is Jesus Christ as prophesied by Isaiah of old. "Today this scripture has been fulfilled in your hearing," Jesus later proclaimed to a shocked group in the synagogue on that day of remix and new birth. They're response? "They got up, drove him out of the town, and led him to the brow of the hill on which their town was built, so that they might hurl him off the cliff." Sound like 'hip hop'?

In truth, we all try and throw Jesus off the cliff throughout our lives, hip hop and not. 'Thug' behavior is not exclusive to one genre or culture. But in the 'remix' and 'rebirth' hip hop comes to tell us anew, to shout out, like Isaiah millennia ago, that Jesus' way can be our way, too. The reconciling love and power of faith is alive into new days and new ways following Jesus in all culture, form and manner.

This is the story of the 'remix' which means 'new life,' and 'new birth.' It ask that we trust in God, 'get clean' and confess our sins, praise and celebrate the Divine in all we do, all we say – all we are. God is the "reason for all season," rhymes the rapper. "Make us new, O God, make us new... Let your people celebrate you, in all we do, in all we do..."

A New Thing: God Gives and Blesses The Remix

Had you told me, an Episcopal priest, trained and educated in the Anglo-Catholic tradition of 'Street and Altar,' that I would one day be a 'Hip Hop Priest,' I might have run off a cliff on my own! "Just your ordinary gay, white, Episcopal, hip hop priest," I have called myself. Not just our liturgy and praise of God, but lives are 're-mixed' and 're-born,' too. We know that as Christians. But how surprising and shocking God's ways can be so often.

The remix is the cycle of life in the faith: from Jesus to the World; from Hebrew Scripture to Paul's writings and teachings; from the tradition of the church in its first fifteen centuries in the West to Luther, Calvin and the English Reformers who, I remind the rappers, gave us the King James Bible and The Book of Common Prayer, both considerable works of remix and new birth. God gives and blesses the remix, from culture to culture, life to life and generation to generation.

HipHopEMass: Friday, June 11, 2004

HipHopEMass has introduced and made familiar the Good News of Jesus Christ to thousands of persons across the United States and World. Hip hop communities have, in just a few years, sprung up North and South, East and West: in Atlantic City, New York, Cincinnati, all across Virginia, a 'Hip Hop Hippo" (St. Augustine of Hippo) in Pennsylvania, a "Hip Hop Chapel" for the incarcerated in Missouri, a parish that presents graduating seniors with the first edition of The Hip Hop Prayer Book just outside Washington, D.C., and through big and small churches and communities in cities and towns all over the country. All opening their hearts and doors to new life in search of the ages-old message of God's Love for All.

Much of this has been made possible through the printed word. Besides this Remix of the original The Hip Hop Prayer Book (2006), we have seen a book of hip hop prayers (The Gathering, released in 2007) and the larger story of our ministry, hip hop, and the Church (Disciples of the Street: The Promise of a Hip Hop Church), published. We have also a wonderful recording of the original music from the HipHopEMass, And the Word Was Hip Hop (2007), available to all. These books and the record are celebrated literally all across the world, in popular literature, on street, and at altar in many faith traditions. And all of this from the words and hearts of the children and young people of hip hop, yesterday and today.

Thousands more have welcomed the rappers, musicians and clergy of HipHopEMass into their home, church, cathedral, street, gymnasium, prison, detention center, park, university or school. HipHopEMass at its core is a mission, and those of us who are a part of it are missionaries, not because of Hip Hop, but for the one hope and love in God, Lover and Maker of All. "One mic, one life, one Love... That's the Power of the Holy Spirit," raps out Freestyle Master and HipHopEMass 'Big Brother,' D.O. ("Defy the Odds"), an editor and contributor of The Remix and The Hip Hop Prayer Book.

HipHopEMass, and the book you hold in your hands, is the celebration of the wonder, love and beauty of GodHipHop. Founded in the Episcopal (Anglican) tradition, HipHopEMass was created as an outreach to the children and young people of the South Bronx neighborhood of Morrisania in the City of New York. HipHopEMass celebrates new ministry, new challenge, new life and new possibilities for church, society and hip hop based in Biblical and (Episcopal) Prayer Book Tradition. The remix of the 'old' word is alive and vibrant at 'Street and Altar' because both are necessary for re-birth and renewal.

The Hip Hop Prayer Book: The Remix is the result of an amazing story being made new itself. A century-and-a-half old parish had begun to dream about more widely opening its doors to the children and young people of its community. Surrounded by two dozen "PJ's" (project high rises) in its infamous neighborhood of the South Bronx, few in the community imagined that seven successive street masses in the summer of 2004, celebrated as the "Trinity Hip Hop Mass," would mean not only the possibility for rebirth of one parish, but perhaps many. HipHopEMass has been honored by the World Council of Churches, the Southern Christian Leadership Conference and Harvard Divinity School, among others, for its work for freedom, justice and peace. The ministry has also been recognized by The New York Times, Newsweek, CNN, Stevie Wonder, national and worldwide media for its mission and vision. "Not your grandfather's church," quipped one national magazine. "Powerful, imaginative worship," said a religious weekly. Black Media Awards honored HipHopEMass with the "Best Christian Youth Ministry Website" (2007).

This work was made possible by the rappers, musicians, writers and worshippers who in only a few years have discovered and re-discovered, mixed and re-mixed a relevant, powerful and beautiful means to love and celebrate God in the idiom and praise of the street. It is no surprise that hip hop today is regarded as one of the single greatest tools of communication not simply among youth, but across generations and cultures worldwide. The vernacular and culture of hip hop represented by HipHopEMass is a positive, forceful tool for evangelism into the 21st century. Positive engagement with hip hop is a mission imperative for the Church, hip hop being the "last form of transcendence available to young black ghetto dwellers," according to Cornell West three decades ago.

The Remix Is Begun

"Remix" is the lifeblood of Hip Hop. "Rebirth" is the new and wondrous life of church and believer, historically, currently, and into the future. Together, through "remix" and "rebirth" – hip hop and the church – we celebrate life and vitality, Love for God and Love for All, and accountability to each other. The Remix and rebirth is life itself, as a believer and a person fully and meaningfully alive to God's Promise. Let the Remix live on, celebrated by young and old, new and traditional, across lines of discord into the unity of the Heart of God. Let the rich heart of soul, the old spiritual, the melodic traditional and dynamism of gospel, deepened by the blues and bejeweled by a little jazz, all come together, re-imagined, reinterpreted and remixed into new days and new ways to the Glory of God. The rappers are the messengers of God! And their message is, following Isaiah, 'God is doing a new thing; do you not see it, feel it, celebrate it – the awesome Love of God, ever new yet ever changeless'?

"To enter the kingdom of heaven, you must be born again," said Jesus in the Gospel. Church, People of God: Are we "born again" into a new day, standing on the promises of old? Or are we hiding from the World and from the Gospel of Jesus Christ? Not so long ago, a small group of believers stepped out of their 'safe' churches onto the streets of the South Bronx to give birth – led by the children and young people – to a ministry and a mission which has made a difference in the lives of many known and many more we do not know except in the spirit of love and gift. That which had been 'thrown away' was built into a cornerstone and it lives on today in countless hearts and lives as "HipHopEMass" remixing a better way for church, society and hip hop.

Do You Celebrate Your Hood?

The story of HipHopEMass is as local as struggling urban parishes and communities trying to see a new day, urban areas where so much of the church has surrendered or faltered in recent decades. It is as international as young prophetic rappers in Marseilles and Paris shouting out for justice; rappers of Brazilian favelas, or slums, working alongside local police to heal and befriend the marginalized; and, African, Central American, Asian and European clergy who have made their pilgrimage to a hip hop mass to celebrate GodHipHop, asking how they can take hip hop worship home only to discover talented rappers at their own 'hoods. HipHopEMass reaches past black/white, young/old, 'new school/old school' dichotomies and boundaries into the hearts of people across political, generational, and faith experience. Hip Hop leads us into a Greater Truth! We are at once new, yet traditional, not alternative, but orthodox in our interpretation, our catholicity, our love and evangelism of the Gospel of Jesus Christ.

Despite its eventual mainstreaming into American commercial culture in the 1980s and 1990s, hip hop was birthed by young outcasts of the Bronx, who saw great highways cut through the borough's heart, neighborhoods being demolished for the convenience of outsiders, and thousands of apartment buildings being burned down by absentee landlords during the infamous "Burning of the Bronx" in the 1970s. The Bronx had become what one observe called, "America's Slum."

In the best of biblical, African American and American civil rights traditions, the children and young people would not surrender. They stood up to celebrate life in the face of flames and destruction, crime, homelessness and poverty. They created hip hop verse and rhyme, which gave them a sense of pride and respect. Since public school provided little in the way of music, dance and art, the children created their own. They "beat-boxed," "break-danced" and expressed their hope to survive in street graffiti. "On one side of the street big buildings would be burning down," recalled Kurtis Blow, the King of Rap and a founder of HipHopEMass, "while kids on the other side would be putting up graffiti messages like, 'Up with Hope. Down with Dope,' 'I Will Survive' and 'Lord Show Me the Way!" We call this "liberation" in our schools of theology. The children and young people called it "rap" and "Hip Hop" (capitalized most often because "Hip Hop is our Nation," taught one rapper). Violence was decried by

Afrika Bambaataa, the Father of Hip Hop Culture, and others who followed him. Gang members were bid to battle only in "rap," dance, and art, not fists, knives, and guns.

Hip Hop became the voice of liberation, a cry of hope against homelessness, against those tearing apart homes, families and whole communities, against greed and hurt. Poet, prophet Tupac Shakur (1972-1996) wrote eloquently about children and young people like him as the "roses that grew from concrete." Many were the roses that grew out of the burned-out high rises and crisscrossed neighborhoods of the Bronx in the 1970s, "when no one even cared," wrote Tupac. There wer few who befriended the children. Fewer still who were their champions. A national presidential administration could only provide ketchup for school meals. Children and young people found what nourishment and hope they could from the concrete and devastation, unlikely in their beauty and promise. These are the children – the "roses" – of hip hop. In this greater context, HipHopEMass was founded in the summer of 2004 during seven successive Friday night street masses that captured the imaginations of many. "Where is all this hip hop coming from, Father Tim?" I would hear. And I would respond, "The question is not where is all this hip hop coming from, but where has the Church been all these years?"

The basis elements of hip hop have remained. Most participants and observers identify five key elements to hip hop: DJing, MCing, dancing (break, step, snap, krump...), graffiti or "hip hop iconography," as we politely call it at HipHopEMass, and cultural style (ranging from clothing and bling to magazines and literature to what rappers we favor and why). As sixth element can be identified as "beatboxing," a form of expression in which a sole performer uses voice and body to make sounds mimicking scratching (as if on a vinyl record), drums, even stereo sounds and other modes of music and music-making. Kurtis Blow, the first rapper to go Gold and our first music director, adds a seventh element: "love and understanding" or "personal spirituality." He says that this is about the way you live your life, the "way you live your Hip Hop!" Hip Hop is a culture that includes much of the culture and context of the South Bronx but also of constituencies and populations throughout America and the world of the 21st century.

Supreme! God Did It!
The Celebration of Remix and New Birth

Everything we do at HipHopEMass centers around the teaching, practice and experience of Holy Scripture (God's Word, the Living Stories of Salvation) leading us to the celebration of Holy Eucharist and Holy Baptism, the two chief sacraments of the Church. Both Holy Eucharist – the Big Celebration - and Holy Baptism are always beautiful, powerful liturgies. "I really feel like I've been to Church," I enjoy hearing. "Sacraments" are defined by The Book of Common Prayer as outward and visible signs of spiritual and inward grace, given by Christ as sure and certain means by which we receive that grace. Whether celebrated at an altar in church or at an altar "on the street," everything begins and ends at God's Holy Table where Christ has commanded us to remember and love God and Neighbor as self.

We take every opportunity at HipHopEMass to teach the Holy Bible and the order of The Book of Common Prayer (Episcopal Tradition) to better define and structure our worship. The Remix and The Hip Hop Prayer Book beautifully represent this goal. We also worship extemporaneously, most typically through Laying on Hands and Prayers and Blessings on Street Corners and places of business and gathering. While MC's, DJ's and rappers lead everything we do in hip hop liturgy, Eucharistic and Baptismal Celebrations are presided over by ordained priests and ministers (both men and women) who consecrate or "bless" bread and wine at table. All other worship services – such as Daily Prayers – are celebrated and led by both clergy and lay (not ordained) persons, quite often the rappers themselves or other leaders of the congregation. All are trained and ably lead. All the People of God are welcome and encouraged to lead and assist in all other celebrations and prayers in both of our liturgical texts, similar though different in a variety of ways.

One of our hip hop communities recently divided weekly services in a workable and popular succession (of about one hour each) as follows:

1st Fridays:	Welcome Concert with Potluck (Goal: Get folks to Church)
2nd Fridays:	Gettin' Clean with Holy Anointing (Goal: Reconciliation and Peace)
3rd Fridays:	Holy Baptism (Goal: Making it real! Don't waste time)
4th Fridays:	Big Celebration + Holy Eucharist (all elements of Hip Hop present)
5th Fridays:	Street Church (rap, prayers, anointing at street corners and gathering places, e.g., barber and beauty shops, basketball courts, Laundromats, outside bodegas, church front doors...)

Schedules and local celebrations need to be carefully designed, well publicized with as many church 'fathers' and 'mothers' present as possible.

The Remix features a lot of rap and rhyme that is new. Much of the Liturgy, or Worship, is the same, though with expanded prayers and sections and a more elegant organization.

Hip Hop Prayer Book: The Remix is broken into four sections.

I.   Prayers accompanied by thematic Psalms
     Individual and Community or Corporate Prayers

II. Worship
     Getting' Clean + Reconciliation, Holy Anointing and
     Holy Eucharist with Prayers for Holy Matrimony and
     Death and Resurrection

III. Word
     Bible Stories from the Family of God – That's Us!
     Rap follows traditional versions

IV. Back-Up
     Several helpful tools to get everything started
     including Sample Orders of Service, a Discography,
     a Glossary and our product information

Those involved in this prayer book have worked hard to make all of the services and prayers "user-friendly" for all people: first-timers as well as seasoned hip hop and traditional church-goers, hip hop fans and not, rappers, rhyme kings and queens and those who find it hard to keep a beat.

We respect and appreciate all of the rappers who – for many, a first – agreed for their words to be set down in writing. Like the oral tradition of the Christian Testament itself, rap is mobile, rapidly changing from and within many cultures and not easily given to the written tradition (much like many faith traditions are not easily given to oral tradition). We learn together. All worshippers and readers are asked, then, to give yourselves and the text time as you pray and enter into the worship of GodHipHop!

We celebrate numerous new rappers and artists in their contributions to The Remix. Many of these artists appeared in the original Hip Hop Prayer Book. We are limited in size and scope of this project which means that talented, wonderful rappers and artists from many HipHopEMass communities – known and unknown – have not been included. God Willing, there will be future projects and celebrations of the gifts that All of Our Rappers bring, however. Our Love and Gratitude to each and every rapper is genuine and long-lasting. Keep shouting out and stay on mission!

What HipHopEMass Is Not

A great American preacher once taught me that the best sermons are sure to say what a sermon is not – in a moment – so that the greater message can be clearly and freely delivered and received. After five years of active ministry among many persons from many places, and having introduced to you who we are, please consider what this ministry is not:

- We do not attempt a re-interpretation or replacement of the Bible or Book of Common Prayer. We hope to illumine and make welcome those persons who have never heard the Bible-story or the words of worship from our liturgy;

- We do not wish to replace or deter from traditional worship or to negate existing parish communities of any form except to add to the baptized and confirmed in the faith;
- We most often augment communities of the faithful, with periodic, weekly or monthly celebrations – we are not singularly 'hip hop' nor do we see God as owned by 'hip hop' or any one vernacular or culture;
- The First and Great Commandment is to Love God with Everything and the Second is to Love Everybody (as Ourselves). We do not tolerate hate or violence of any kind, in word or deed, both within out own community or anywhere else;
- We are not only African-American, children or young. Hip Hop is today the world's number one music genre. We represent practically all cultures and we celebrate and are celebrated by all generations;
- We are not merely 'urban' but city, town and country. The suburbs are the major buyer of popular hip hop – about 70% of the genre is sold the suburban youth, an important marketing statistic from which the church can learn;
- HipHopEMass builds up community and heritage. We are not anti-cultural and welcome people of all faiths and traditions or those with no faith at all;
- Hip Hop is not the answer to church mission, redevelopment and planting, but an answer. Hip Hop celebrates many constituencies as the leading art and music form in the 21st century; and,
- We are not a 'fad' or 'curiosity'. We are not 'entertainment'. HipHopEMass is worship, High Altar and Low, inside and out, lost and redeemed, locked-up and free. We are 're-born' to and 're-mixed in' the Love of God everyday.

Twelve Rules for Good Hip Hop Worship

1. Experience a hip hop mass or liturgy – stay in touch through HipHopEMass.org.

2. Pray in the vernacular of hip hop – do not be afraid!

3. Listen to the rap of the 'street' – it knows what's good and what's not.

4. Be genuine in all you do – the children and young people will love you.

5. Know your 'hood – its history, needs, capabilities and make-up – Walk the Parish!

6. Respond with focused, ongoing, person-to-person outreach – Stand Tall!

7. Life is change – do not fear. Hold fast to that which is good. Chunk the rest.

8. Celebrate the creativity of Hip Hop – in song, dance, rap, word and life.

9. Remix favorite old hymns and melodies with a hip hop beat. Yes! Yes! Y'All!

10. 'Call and Response' is the new rubric – discover and live more freely!

11. Use 'hooks' – refrain – in response – everywhere cuz God's Love Don't Stop.

12. The Orthodox pray with icons. We Anglicans with many books. Hip Hop loves its beats – get to know and appreciate a beat-maker!

Amen. WORD!

Work, give and pray for new days, new ways in thanksgiving for all the generations of Christ, all past, all present and all to come. I use this following prayer ever more frequently from The Book of Common Prayer in hip hop and traditional ministry. I am praying and asking for vocations for leadership for the Church from all over the world. I pray in Great Joy for the Remix of Life, for the Love God and for the Children and Young People who bless this world beyond all knowledge and expectation. Pray with me:

THE COLLECT FOR ORDINATIONS

O God of unchangeable power and light: Look favorably upon your whole Church, that wonderful and sacred mystery; by the effectual working of your providence, carry out in tranquility the plan of salvation; let the whole world see and know that things which were cast down are being raised up, and things which had grown old are being made new, and that all things are being brought to their perfection by him through whom all things were made, your Son Jesus Christ our Lord: who lives and reigns with you, in the unity of the Holy Spirit, one God, for ever and ever.

Amen. WORD!

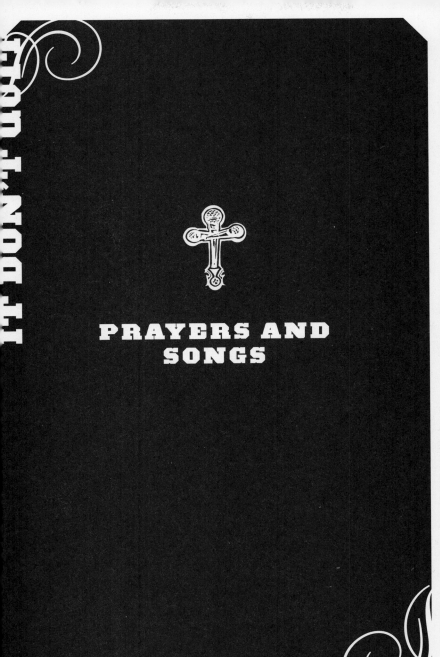

PRAYERS AND
SONGS

Prayers 4 Adoration and Praise

Venite, exultemus + Psalm 95

God gets all props
*   Rejoice until your voice and your back bows out*
*   He made the map flat out*
Tied it together with his own two
*   I'm prone to — praise wherever that I roam to*
It might be the mountains that he sculpted
It might be the deep sea because he own it
*   We like sheep; we might choke on our own spit*
If he hadn't timed it, he's quick with the Heimlich
I might sit in the master's pasture,
*   Rest while he expresses past disasters*
"Them cats was bad kids.
The wilderness crew.
*   Talk until you're blue they ain't gone listen to you*
And so I gave'm a few — years to work it out
Like jerks they doubted me and it irks me now
To reminisce, reminisce on their ignorance
*   Because of this, them and their kids could never sit in bliss."*

Come, let us sing to the Lord;
    let us shout for joy to the Rock of our salvation.
Let us come before his presence with thanksgiving
    and raise a loud shout to him with psalms.
For the Lord is a great God,
    and a great King above all gods.
In his hand are the caverns of the earth,
    and the heights of the hills are his also.

The sea is his, for he made it,
  and his hands have molded the dry land.
Come, let us bow down, and bend the knee,
  and kneel before the Lord our Maker.
For he is our God,
and we are the people of his pasture and the sheep of his hand.
  Oh, that today you would hearken to his voice!
Harden not your hearts,
as your forebears did in the wilderness,
  at Meribah, and on that day at Massah,
  when they tempted me.
They put me to the test,
  though they had seen my works.
Forty years long I detested that generation and said,
  "This people are wayward in their hearts;
  they do not know my ways."
So I swore in my wrath,
  "They shall not enter into my rest."

AMEN. WORD!

Jubilate Deo + Psalm 100

Let's have some have some hype y'all
  Let's have some hoopla
God's the truth y'all
  He such a superstar
He held out two hands
He held out two paws
  And made us same as his greatness, with a few flaws
That way we'll stay in the gate cause he's the true Boss
  He hopes that you toss
All you cares off
Before you step to his door or don't you dare cross
  We gotta give him recognition like a Blair Cross
And I'm gone wanna to hug and kiss him til the airs off
  yeah I'm gone wanna hug and kiss him til the airs off

Be joyful in the Lord, all you lands;
    serve the Lord with gladness
    and come before his presence with a song.
Know this: The Lord himself is God;
    he himself has made us, and we are his;
    we are his people and the sheep of his pasture.
Enter his gates with thanksgiving;
go into his courts with praise;
    give thanks to him and call upon his Name.
For the Lord is good;
his mercy is everlasting;
    and his faithfulness endures from age to age.

THE LORD IS ALL THAT

Psalm 149

Let's give it up to God... that's where it's at
    So we gotta give it up with a brand new rap
Let all Israel celebrate the creator
    Holdin it down
with the utmost flavah

Let's dance, move our feet and put our hands together
    Cause God got our back forever and ever
Let's make some noise, scream and Holla!
    Let's give it up for the heavenly father
Some aren't down, so they stray and defy
    With so much that you do can only wonder why
Some are hardheaded, you can't tell them nothin'
    But they'll understand when you make your judgment
That's when they find themselves in drama
    And all those who love God are in the seat of honor!

Hallelujah!
Sing to the Lord a new song;
    sing his praise in the congregation of the faithful.

Let Israel rejoice in his Maker;
>	let the children of Zion be joyful in their King.
Let them praise his Name in the dance;
>	let them sing praise to him with timbrel and harp.
For the Lord takes pleasure in his people
>	and adorns the poor with victory.
Let the faithful rejoice in triumph;
>	let them be joyful on their beds.
Let the praises of God be in their throat
>	and a two-edged sword in their hand;
To wreak vengeance on the nations
>	and punishment on the peoples;
To bind their kings in chains
>	and their nobles with links of iron;
To inflict on them the judgment decreed;
>	this is glory for all his faithful people.
>	Hallelujah!

GOD'S LOVE DON'T STOP

U-N-B-E-L-I-E-V-A-B-L-E!

You love us so much; we're not knowing what to do with it,
You're everlasting no danger of us ever losing it,
You produce a paradise we had to run and ruin it
You had one Son; we hung him on a crucifix
Still you love, still you forgive, still there's mercy
Every person gets the privelege of living and we're unworthy
You're perfect you put the sun into service and call it early
So it's sunrise in Singapore, midnight in Jersey
You're faster than Michael Irvin, more Diesel than Vin,
You're every artist easel; you're every poet's pen
You're so intense, it don't make sense
Like the highway 85 on the way to Lenox
You can't control the traffic in Atlanta when you drive
I can't believe his tactics he's uncanny all the time
Remnant ranting with this rhyme under one common thesis

We just can't believe ya Jesus!

It's like one of those days; where old age goes both ways
And you're sick of feeling like its all work and no play
For low pay sitting in the same old place
Being greeted by different versions of the same old face
The whole day your simply wishing you could say go away
But not today you awake and realize you're so late
It's like you can't catch no breaks as a working stiff,
Your mouth is permanently shaped like the top half of a circle is
Nervousness clutches as ya catch your boss eyeing ya
Long story short, you got fired bruh
Now you're walking home wondering how beautiful the day is
In this business casual suit you always hated
When was the last time you appreciated the day
And actually saw the sun shine before it faded away
Before you can think about it and without a cloud in the sky,
The rain starts pouring and you thank God for it — it's unbelievable.

What's greater? Is it mercy, love, grace, or healing?
That's an ongoing debate like "Tastes great! Less filling!"
I've been willing to try my best suppress feelings,
But can only hold so much before it starts spilling.
Revealing itself in my actions and speech
Christ bridges the gap between my practice and preach,
That's why I'm bubbling beneath, it's cause of his loving-kindness,
His constant attention, his perfect refinement
I know a gang of cats pretend like they don't have hurt within,
But I was once submerged in sin, and stand opposed like shirts to skins
And we'll never make amends, not as long as grace abounds,
I'll just stand as a man, complete as fertile ground
Let his righteousness resound, I'm about to shout
Cause every time I tried to exit, He was there like Waffle House
Paramount in position, He's got it on lock,
Its Jesus, Ripley's Believe it or Not!

—*remnant*

The Reason Why I Sing

I love to be happy
to be happy that is the reason why I sing
Just to feel the peace and joy it brings
That is the reason why I sing
And when I'm feeling shy and scared, and think of my great song
All my shyness and fears are swept away, and my sadness gone.
God makes me sing
Just to put happiness and love in me.
God loves me with all His heart and soul
That's the reason that I sing

At times I may be shy.
But when I sing to God he grants to me
the strength to breathe and carry on.
Someone may be asking
why I am so shy.
What I'm trying to say through these few words
is that I am just a private guy.

But most importantly, I must be sure you all know this
when I lift my head up high and sing,
God helps me to fly up unto him,
the reason why I sing.

Prayers 4 Thanksgiving

Psalm 85

It's like you smiled at us, made up your mind
  To lift the cloud of doubt and bring back good times
Turned back your threats, calmed your temper
  All we ask is your help, don't hold a grudge forever

We know you were mad, had a right to be vexed
*   Why not start over and resurrect?*
Then we can joke, party and jam
*   Can't wait to hear what you have planned*
Everybody bobbin their head to the beat
*   When love and truth meet on the street*
And there is no more battles, no more war
*   Put down their guns and forgot what they were fightin' for*
Now justice has been restored
*   And we owe it all to you, all powerful Lord!*
Down for your people from the hills to the hood
*   God is great! Now it's all good*

You have been gracious to your land, O Lord,
    you have restored the good fortune of Jacob.
You have forgiven the iniquity of your people
    and blotted out all their sins.
You have withdrawn all your fury
    and turned yourself from your wrathful indignation.
Restore us then, O God our Savior;
    let your anger depart from us.
Will you be displeased with us for ever?
    will you prolong your anger from age to age?
Will you not give us life again,
    that your people may rejoice in you?
Show us your mercy, O Lord,
    and grant us your salvation.
I will listen to what the Lord God is saying,
    for he is speaking peace to his faithful people
    and to those who turn their hearts to him.
Truly, his salvation is very near to those who fear him,
    that his glory may dwell in our land.
Mercy and truth have met together;
    righteousness and peace have kissed each other.
Truth shall spring up from the earth,
    and righteousness shall look down from heaven.

The Lord will indeed grant prosperity,
and our land will yield its increase.
Righteousness shall go before him,
and peace shall be a pathway for his feet.

God's Love Don't Stop + Psalm 136

God we give thanks "Your love don't stop."
Your on top of all Gods "Your love don't stop."
The Lord of all lords "Your love don't stop."
Miracles you work for "Your love don't stop."
You made the constellations "Your love don't stop."
Earth and Ocean foundations "Your love don't stop."
Filled the sky with light "Your love don't stop."
Sunny days moon at night "Your love don't stop."
Stop the top males in Egypt "Your love don't stop."
Now Israel is free cause "Your love don't stop."
How did the Red Sea split? "Your love don't stop."
And Israel proceed in "Your love don't stop."
Kept us from Pharaoh "Your love don't stop."
Deserts and Parole "Your love don't stop."
Who bombs on Acolytes "Your love don't stop."
Sihon and Amorite "Your love don't stop."
Og and Bashanite "Your love don't stop."
Gives Israel the fight "Your love don't stop."
Saves us when we're down "Your love don't stop."
When haters try to clown "Your love don't stop."
In our time of need "Your love don't stop."
He's God and indeed, Your love don't stop
"Your love don't stop."

Give thanks to the Lord, for he is good,
for his mercy endures for ever.
Give thanks to the God of gods,
for his mercy endures for ever.

Give thanks to the Lord of Lords,
>   for his mercy endures for ever.
Who only does great wonders,
>   for his mercy endures for ever;
Who by wisdom made the heavens,
>   for his mercy endures for ever;
Who spread out the earth upon the waters,
>   for his mercy endures for ever;
Who created great lights,
>   for his mercy endures for ever;
The sun to rule the day,
>   for his mercy endures for ever;
The moon and the stars to govern the night,
>   for his mercy endures for ever.
Who struck down the firstborn of Egypt,
>   for his mercy endures for ever;
And brought out Israel from among them,
>   for his mercy endures for ever;
With a mighty hand and a stretched-out arm,
>   for his mercy endures for ever;
Who divided the Red Sea in two,
>   for his mercy endures for ever;
And made Israel to pass through the midst of it,
>   for his mercy endures for ever;
But swept Pharaoh and his army into the Red Sea,
>   for his mercy endures for ever;
Who led his people through the wilderness,
>   for his mercy endures for ever.
Who struck down great kings,
>   for his mercy endures for ever;
And slew mighty kings,
>   for his mercy endures for ever;
Sihon, king of the Amorites,
>   for his mercy endures for ever;
And Og, the king of Bashan,
>   for his mercy endures for ever;

And gave away their lands for an inheritance,
    for his mercy endures for ever;
An inheritance for Israel his servant,
    for his mercy endures for ever.
Who remembered us in our low estate,
    for his mercy endures for ever;
And delivered us from our enemies,
    for his mercy endures for ever;
Who gives food to all creatures,
    for his mercy endures for ever.
Give thanks to the God of heaven,
    for his mercy endures for ever.

SUPREME! GOD DID IT.

Happiness

I'm happy God blessed us with songs this world can feel
Or how he blessed missionary men's lyrical skills

Or how he wakes me up in the morning to a meal
Or how my girl sends me love letters in the mail

I'm happy I'm a black man that never went to jail
Family members coming together paying off my bail

I'm happy I can get to heaven, though I live in hell
And if I'm walking with the lord I know I can prevail

I'm happy cause when I was lost you're the one I found lord
And you're the only one that turns my frown upside down and,
With the volume of stupidity turned down

How sweet the sound.

When I was hurt you would talk with me
You always stay the same you would never turn shifty
I can't wait till the day that you come get me

In the street
In the house
In my car
On the job
All alone
Lord I think about my happiness
When I sing
When I dance
As I pray
As I stand
Woo lord I think about my happiness

When I'm happy I envision the streams and the meadows
Sun beaming through the clouds with that beautiful yellow
This feeling is great

I can't describe this beautiful taste
Our father in heaven please don't take this feeling away

When I travel in this world through the storms with no sail
I protected by his hand cause I know that it won't fail

Happiness is when I live the next day to see the sun rise
Or when God's son died the third day his son raised

What would happiness be without our father in heaven?
Would the earth still turn?
Would I still be living?
Whenever I sin

Would the father still be forgiven?
Or will he turn us all away and say that heaven's forbidden

Listen,
Laughter does the heart good like a medicine

I was on fire alive now I'm dead again
Need to open up the bible and get feed again
Read what the lord said again and go tell a friend

I was doing good but then I fell again
Me and the lord we talk late night like david letterman
I try to be a better man
And every time I need help I pray please lord lend a hand
Then he comes down and helps enough wealth
He blesses me with food shelter enough health

I had enough of self
I took the failed route
Sin in jail now but the lord got me bailed out

Now I rejoice cause I'm happy
Now I rejoice whenever I see Satan coming at me

He can't faze me no more
Play me no more
Raise the sword
God children say praise the lord

—*Missionary Men (Jahdiel Numan Puello, Eric Monk)*

Prayers 4 Confession

Lord it's hard bein' locked up
I hear demons talking but I wanna interrupt.
With all of these burdens sittin on my chest—
It's hard to carry on, so father, may I rest?
With chains around my body, things are getting heavy.
Can prayin every day really save a human's soul?
**So Lord don't let my spirit go, this is something my body as a
    fallen angel!**

You've put me through some hell in my life,
But I keep my head because I know I'll survive & realize—
And when I'm gone will my spirit still carry on?
I keep the things hurtin deep inside and try to hide my true
    feelin's.
Lord I need healin' because the devils all over my back
I don't want to do wrong, that I know for a fact.
I'm not a boy anymore I'm a man.
Here on Earth I'm tryna do my best.
So I'll continue to try.
So Lord don't let this spirit but this but this is something my
    heart knows
As a fallen angel.

—*Incarcerated Youth, USA*

GOD IS GREAT. GOD IS GOOD.

Will You Remember Me?

Luke 23: 26-43

Jesus, Jesus
Will you remember me?
I need from today
Until eternity

Forgive me, God
I done wrong, God
My life's a mess, God
I must confess God

What a sight to see
You don't wanna be me
I'm hangin' on a tree
For all the world to see

What a criminal I am
And I've spent my life

Gettin' out of jams
And now here I am

Convicted of my crimes
And I've spent my life
Gettin' out of jams
And now here I am

Convicted of my crimes
And I've paid the price
Now I'm doin' my time
This cross don't feel right

As I look around
I see plenty
Of thugs who done wrong
But their crosses are empty

I've got my cross
Nailed to my hands
I bears the weight
Of all my sins

Man, what happened to my plans

Look, two more criminals
Hang on their own
One's a thug
And one, I don't know

They call him Jesus
And his only crime
Was that he came from God
And that he was divine

They don't treat me as bad
As they treat him

And I have to laugh
Cause I'm the one with the sin

They mock and call him
As the king of the Jews
But Jesus said
To forgive what they do

Jesus, I'm a thug
On this cross I belong
But you Jesus
You done nothing wrong

Then he turns to me
With love in his eyes
He said today you will be with me
In paradise

Paradise, that sounds nice
Paradise, that's the price
And then he died
And I cried
And said...

Jesus, Jesus
Will you remember me?
I need from today
Until eternity

Forgive me, God
I done wrong, God
My life's a mess, God
I must confess God

—*Rap Rev Maribebop*

I've did some bad things in my life,
from getting high to bad fights.
Plus lying, stealing & getting nice.
I knew that all those things weren't right.
But now I have Jesus to make things tight.
I will never betray God for the devil ever again.
Well, I can't say never, but I'll strive not to sin.

—*Incarcerated Youth, USA*

LET'S SHOW GOD SOME LOVE!

God is Here

I am a unique expression of God's essence
My bodily temple is a temporary residence
My spirit's nomadic
And no matter where it travels it's charismatic
Nobody's perfect but God is here
To guide us through the seconds, minutes, months and years
Faith and love replace doubt and fear
Nobody's perfect but God is here

I am a divine being
And I prefer the sound of laughing to the sound of screaming
All-knowing, all-seeing, all loving
Stuffed in the body of a human being
Bruised and beaten from the ego
It follows us around everywhere we go
Shows us what's wrong with each other
And helps us judge the actions of another
All creation has purpose
There's no way anything is worthless
Every mistake is a blessing
So please, forgive yourself and stop stressing
Everything you need is on its way
Every single day, in every single way
Delivery, precisely on time in
Amounts so large it'll blow your mind

Reason to believe the ego deceives
Probable Cause, it's the cause of greed
Everything I need is on its way
Every single day so I often pray
G-O-D, help me see
Help me be what you need from me
Give me the power to seek you
Recognize you and know you too
I'm a divine tool, creation with purpose
That purpose is for what I've been searching
My purpose is to be like God
That's my only hobby, that's my only job
The rest of the stress doesn't even exist
From the viewpoint of the infinite
The ego stays in a lake of fire
We were created to stay inspired

—*Brandon C. Stephens*

AMEN. WORD!

I Feel

I'm lost in my own misery
I don't know which way to go,
or which path to choose, I'm bound
to win, but I feel I'm bound to lose.
Why do I feel this way, who knows?
But I do know every time I close my eyez
my brain glows, it tells me 2 move, but I
always stand still, because man I feel,
crome stone man steel. "Boy to Man," the years
have flew, his growth has grew, and his mind
is constantly searching for "new." He choses
to rise out of physical aggression. I will
show passion. I will show love, not hate.
Positive can "chill" but negativity is looking for
"bait." I won't provide that bait, I provided enough.

I was standing with the title of positive actions.
No I'm at the bluff of a flow.
I feel I've lost power, within myself, and
within my friends, Lost can it ever lose, because
I won't let it win.
I chose not to sin.
It must be terminated.
It is no longer my friend.
I'm desperate to change ways,
like the world changes days.
As I awake, I steer from eyez
that look from the skies, as
it begins to daze
people look at my picture
and read the phrase,
"so I've chosen
some bad ways."
But closed my palms and I prayed.

—*Donay Davis*

Prayers 4 Intercession

Psalm 121

When I get weak, and want to be a coward
  He gives me the strength, gives me the power
Keeps me strong, keeps me diesel
  He's unbelievable

When I was in the gym, I thought it came from weights
  Then I realized where I got my strength
Wasn't from skyscrapers, or buildings in the sky
  Wasn't from how hard I worked, or how many times I tried
Wasn't no pain / no gain, the saying that I heard

It came from the one that made the heavens and the Earth
It came from GOD, came from the Word
That was made Flesh, all I had to do was observe
No need to worry, no need to fret
God was right by my side, standin' to protect
Guard me from evil and any danger
Rollin with GOD, have nothing to be afraid of!

I lift up my eyes to the hills;
    from where is my help to come?
My help comes from the Lord,
    the maker of heaven and earth.
He will not let your foot be moved
    and he who watches over you will not fall asleep.
Behold, he who keeps watch over Israel
    shall neither slumber nor sleep;
The Lord himself watches over you;
    the Lord is your shade at your right hand,
So that the sun shall not strike you by day,
    nor the moon by night.
The Lord shall preserve you from all evil;
    it is he who shall keep you safe.
The Lord shall watch over your going out and your coming in,
    from this time forth for evermore.

THE LORD IS ALL THAT

Psalm 130

Help me God… I'm callin out to you
I'm fallin apart and don't know what to do
Feel like I'm up against it all by myself
Can you hear me plead, my cries for help
Listen to my story; I hope you can hear me
I'm prayin out to you, to see if you'll respond
Say my prayer at night, and wait till the dawn
Wait and I watch lookin for your arrival
Sometimes I feel like it's my only way of survival

So I pray on my knees and I look up above
Cause I know, with your arrival comes love
I'm going to keep going and keep up my faith
Cause I know that you're comin and on your way!

Out of the depths have I called to you, O Lord;
Lord, hear my voice;
    let your ears consider well the voice of my supplication.
If you, Lord, were to note what is done amiss,
    O Lord, who could stand?
For there is forgiveness with you;
    therefore you shall be feared.
I wait for the Lord; my soul waits for him;
    in his word is my hope.
My soul waits for the Lord,
more than watchmen for the morning,
    more than watchmen for the morning.
O Israel, wait for the Lord,
    for with the Lord there is mercy;
With him there is plenteous redemption,
    and he shall redeem Israel from all their sins.

GOD'S LOVE DON'T STOP

Emancipation

There's a devastation in our nation
A ball of confusion, we need a Church revolution
To deliberate is the antidote, disciple the word
Haven't ya heard, Oh no we're blinded
It's time to heavenly reminded
Like King I have a dream
The Gospel is received and believe
From the start just depart from the evil one
Stick a fork in Satan cause the succa's done
Turn to God's son, no more guns
Let the cross saturate and penetrate a cha heart

Cause at the cross he suffered and bled from the start
And died, and the blood had to be supplied
To purify us thus he was crucified
That the most despicable sins could be justified
Sanctimonious hypocrisy is a mockery
And contrary to the vary truth about Calvary
It won't suffice for the price of the sacrifice
Paid by Christ, it's time to share the Gospel with the
    whole generation
Emancipation of a Nation

—*Kurtis Blow and C. Money*

THAT'S WHAT'S UP

Searchin 4 Change

Where I'm from it's like change never gone come
Cuz dudes rather bust their gunz and get their fundz
Drop outta school play and rap in fact
Especially if the kid Hispanic or Black
I'm just speakin the facts and the truth do hurt
But I know about the pain underneath the shirt
And in your heart is where you go berserk
But God is in my vision, that's why I'm so alert
Faith I can't let go
There's gotta be hope
Prayer is my emotional savior
So when you at rock bottom and no one around 2 help you
You gotta home and it feels like a shelter
Just know that God's near you
But God is in my vision, that's why I'm so alert
Faith I can't let go
There's gotta be hope

—*Glory*

SUPREME! GOD DID IT.

B-L-E-S-S-E-D

Matthew 5: Beatitudes

B-l-e-s-s-e-d, what does it mean to be blessed by thee?
B-l-e-s-s-e-d, blessings are the same for you and me

If you read the Bible then you will see
That blessin's have been handed down in history

And if you keep readin you'll start believing
That you situation is not uncommon

If you've been poor or you wanted to cry
If you feel meek then you side with the weak

You see Jesus came in the same way
He came in the form of a-bay-bay

To help the persecuted and say it's ok
He suffered and he did it every day

So bless-ed are you when you get insulted
Humble yourself and you'll be exalted

For yours is the kingdom and all of it's glory
If you want to know God just keep reading the stories

The good book is written as a guide to do right
But God knows our ways, in the dark he sees light

So rejoice and be glad our reward is in heaven
Blessed in God's arms is where we'll be restin

B-l-e-s-s-e-d, day in day our
God is victory.

—*Rev. Marisol Ferrer*

Prayers 4 Petition

Psalm 116

I was askin for so much, I got it confused...
Shouldn't ask what you can do for me...
It should be, what I can do for you!
Cause you have been down with me for the longest
    So I gotta give it back, complete my promise!
I love GOD cause he listened to me
Listened, as I begged for mercy
    Listened, as I told him bout my story
Lookin for help, but didn't know where to turn
    That's when I would come to learn
That God is gracious; his love is out of site
    Cause God has the power to make all things right!
Realized I could rest, I could relax
    Been showered with blessings, God's had my back
When I realized it, I was more than determined
    He's given so much, I want to be his servant
Been so true to me, been so honest
    Want to do it up for him, and complete my promise!

I love the Lord, because he has heard the voice of my supplication,
    because he has inclined his ear to me whenever
I called upon him.
The cords of death entangled me;
the grip of the grave took hold of me;
    I came to grief and sorrow.
Then I called upon the Name of the Lord:
    "O Lord, I pray you, save my life."
Gracious is the Lord and righteous;
    our God is full of compassion.
The Lord watches over the innocent;
    I was brought very low, and he helped me.

Turn again to your rest, O my soul,
    for the Lord has treated you well.
For you have rescued my life from death,
    my eyes from tears, and my feet from stumbling.
I will walk in the presence of the Lord
    in the land of the living.
I believed, even when I said,
"I have been brought very low."
    In my distress I said, "No one can be trusted."
How shall I repay the Lord
    for all the good things he has done for me?
I will lift up the cup of salvation
    and call upon the Name of the Lord.
I will fulfill my vows to the Lord
    in the presence of all his people.
Precious in the sight of the Lord
    is the death of his servants.
O Lord, I am your servant;
    I am your servant and the child of your handmaid;
    you have freed me from my bonds.
I will offer you the sacrifice of thanksgiving
    and call upon the Name of the Lord.
I will fulfill my vows to the Lord
    in the presence of all his people,
In the courts of the Lord's house,
    in the midst of you, O Jerusalem.
    Hallelujah!

GOD IS GREAT. GOD IS GOOD.

Psalm 129

They try to put me on blast!
(This is an Israel song)
    They try to put me on blast, they've been hate'n for so long
Ever since I was young they kick'n me down
    Whip'n me on the farm try'n to get me to plow
And look at me now, my back is smitten
    But yo' God is with me, he'll attack their city

Until they're black and gritty, like a withered crop
  The kind you quickly chop
Let us lift thee God

"Greatly have they oppressed me since my youth,"
  let Israel now say;
"Greatly have they oppressed me since my youth,
  but they have not prevailed against me."
The plowmen plowed upon my back
  and made their furrows long.
The Lord, the Righteous One,
  has cut the cords of the wicked.
Let them be put to shame and thrown back,
  all those who are enemies of Zion.
Let them be like grass upon the housetops,
  which withers before it can be plucked;
Which does not fill the hand of the reaper,
  nor the bosom of him who binds the sheaves;
So that those who go by say not so much as,
"The Lord prosper you.
  We wish you well in the Name of the Lord."

LET'S SHOW GOD SOME LOVE!

Take the crooked out the cop so the justice is served
no more leaving wrong accused people dead on the curb
Money got u killin flesh & blood with no hesitation
why your boy there take your freedom telling cops information
Tell me why we got 2 cry, if it's bringing us pain
tell me why the most hated weather always the rain
God please save my soul, pain attach my flesh
all this drama can't take it & and it's causing this stress
Make me want 2 put the pistol in my mouth & just squeeze
hope the lord come & get me once I fall to my knees
All this killin all this blood, I don't need 2 see that
I don't want 2 watch my back for something that I regret

—*Incarcerated Youth, USA*

Prayer for the City

God, bless the streets; from the cracks in the concrete
To the feet of police on the beat
They try to keep the peace in these stressful times
Please help us see, give sight to the blind
We think selling drugs is an easy dime
Bless the single mother making bucks in a back alley
Thinking that's how to feed her family
God, please bless the fiend
Fill his heart up with what he really needs
Please, make it know to the people with no home that
You love them and they're never alone
Bless the corner stores and the barbershops, and the
MCs that rap overtop of beat box
God, bless the hearts of the people in the city
Help us see that life is pretty

—*Brandon C. Stephens*

AMEN. WORD!

Inside Boo

The way I feel,
I feel like a dime.
When I don't, I feel like nobody
I feel like I'm not there, or I feel
out of control.

I feel like I want to talk.
No one listens.
I just wanted someone to listen
when I talk, I cry sometimes.

But sometimes I stay strong.

—*Betty Diaz*

Mary Magdalene

Let's see, Mary Magdalene
Where do we begin?
Do we begin with her sin
Or do we end where she begins?

Let's see let's see
Ahhhh, this is how it be...

Jesus had a little lamb
'Twas Mary of this I know
And every where that Jesus went
Mary was sure to go

She followed him to calvary
Where they put him on a tree
I hope you know the rest of this
'Cause she went down in history

You see she led a life of fear
Showing no direction
But God chose her to be a witness
Of his life and resurrection

And when Jesus breathed his last breath
Guess what? Mary was there to see
That Jesus conquered even death
And he achieved our victory

So the next time you are feeling down
Remember Mary Magdalene's life
Focus your eyes on the only one
The resurrected Jesus Christ

—*Rap Rev Maribebop*

Prayers 4 Family

Psalm 67

Master be merciful manifest grace
Mold and make us as models of your face
Acquaint us with your way Jahway
You're a balm in every lawn across all yard gates
We holler "Halle" give palm praise
Wave our hands and feet
Let every nation be glad and sing
Your majesty is more than the average King
Great and gorgeous God, really ravishing
Make every pasture peak
Fields yield increase
Your autograph should be, sealed in me
Praise to your name across the hills and sea
Praise to your name across the hill and sea

May God be merciful to us and bless us,
    show us the light of his countenance and come to us.
Let your ways be known upon earth,
    your saving health among all nations.
Let the peoples praise you, O God;
    let all the peoples praise you.
Let the nations be glad and sing for joy,
    for you judge the peoples with equity
    and guide all the nations upon earth.
Let the peoples praise you, O God;
    let all the peoples praise you.
The earth has brought forth her increase;
    may God, our own God, give us his blessing.

May God give us his blessing,
    and may all the ends of the earth stand in awe of him.

THE LORD IS ALL THAT

Prayer for Family

We say a prayer for our families, we pray for their safety
This is for the fathers, mothers and the babies
We pray for the young sistah's and the young brotha's
For those doing it on their own, for all the single mothers
You are not alone, may God bless you
For the babymamas and fathers just tryin to get thru
Livin' day by day this is why we pray
Have no fear... everythings' gon' be okay!

—D.O.

GOD'S LOVE DON'T STOP

Prayer for the Founders of Hip Hop

ALL LOVE AND HONOR TO AFRIKA BAMBAATAA,
FOUNDER OF HIP HOP CULTURE SBX ⚹ USA!

We pray for our pioneers who brought us this beautiful gift
Without your work, Hip Hop would never exist
We pray that we will learn the message that you taught to us
Didn't have instruments, didn't have lessons, but you didn't fight
    and fuss
You made something from nothing, made it bumpin, bringin the
    noise
You moved the crowd, and did it loud, and you found your voice
For guiding us, for inspiring us, more than you'll ever know
For resurrecting us connecting us, takin it around the globe
For your creativity, ingenuity, for bringing us Hip Hop
And we will continue on cause it don't quit and it don't stop

—D.O.

Prayer for the Rappers

To the man of upstairs,
  Ups for the rappers who give a shout out in your name,
   For the temple that praises you and keeps us all sane,
    Let their words be a part of the backbeat of our lives and theirs
Keeping them in rythm with you. Word.
—*The Rev. Lynne Washington and the youngins at the*
  Peter Paul Development Center, Richmond, Virginia

THAT'S WHAT'S UP

Prayer for DJs

ALL LOVE ✦ HONOR TO COOL CLYDE ✦ LIGHTNIN LANCE, SBX ✦ USA
1ST TO SCRATCH WAX WORLDWIDE!

Dear God
Please look over our DJs, on the ones and twos
Who keep the party rocking and make the crowd move
They take our worry and troubles away
By every phat cut they play
Your love for us is like when they drop the needle
Makin it happen, scratchin, it's Unbelieveable!
Getting it together, makin it transform
Cause like you,
The party don't start till yall come on
So we pray for the DJs and the pioneers
For keeping it live and bringin flava in ya ear!
—D.O.

SUPREME! GOD DID IT.

Prayer for Hip Hop eMass

It started with the Word,
from all our hearts, heard
Burstin with the joy in life,
the truth is first,

Hip hop made what
the word Is
God give us this street
So we unify with you like
like Cursive
E for everybody,
all together
with one purpose
Give us the rythm
to make the rhymes,
shine for your service.
Let us make us what we are
The Lord moves us.
We pray to make us selfless,
remove us from what we think makes us,
so we can rap thus,
whats real,
and untainted.

—*Tripp Levine*

Prayers  Community

Psalm 46

God is our refuge. If troubles test you
    He's who you step to
We kept cool when the high tides swept through
    And the earthquake shakes right and left moves
We bless you!

There's an estuary, that rests very high
    With a river in the middle set by El Shaddai
Kept wet, never dry
    Its water runs before the sun hits the sky
    And with one little cry....

Heathen schemes seem really weak and
he brings kingdoms to their knees and
Humiliates them
So we praise him, God of Jacob.
Hey kids, ladies gents, attention please
He who plants seeds and keeps the peace
From the West to East
By break'n weaponry over his chest and knees
Has requested your attention please heed his speech
"Stop and See that I preside over every rock and tree."

I'll try not to be faithless
It's he who made us.
God of Jacob

God is our refuge and strength,
     a very present help in trouble.
Therefore we will not fear, though the earth be moved,
     and though the mountains be toppled into the
     depths of the sea;
Though its waters rage and foam,
     and though the mountains tremble at its tumult.
The Lord of hosts is with us;
     the God of Jacob is our stronghold.
There is a river whose streams make glad the city of God,
     the holy habitation of the Most High.
God is in the midst of her;
she shall not be overthrown;
     God shall help her at the break of day.
The nations make much ado, and the kingdoms are shaken;
     God has spoken, and the earth shall melt away.
The Lord of hosts is with us;
     the God of Jacob is our stronghold.
Come now and look upon the works of the Lord,
     what awesome things he has done on earth.
It is he who makes war to cease in all the world;
     he breaks the bow, and shatters the spear,

and burns the shields with fire.
"Be still, then, and know that I am God;
    I will be exalted among the nations;
    I will be exalted in the earth."
The Lord of hosts is with us;
    the God of Jacob is our stronghold.

GOD IS GREAT. GOD IS GOOD.

Prayer for Community

Let us say a prayer for the community
Help us see through our differences and come together in unity
We pray for our families and also our neighbors
Protect them from harm and any danger
Give us the strength to help if they are in problems
Give us the guidance so we can try to solve them
Let's look out for our neighbors kids like our parents used ta'
Let our children be the leaders of the future

—D.O.

LET'S SHOW GOD SOME LOVE!

Prayer for the Church

ALL LOVE AND HONOR TO ALL HIP HOP BISHOPS, PRIESTS AND DEACONS

We pray to God, and we also pray for the church
For understanding our message, and helping us do our work
For giving us a place, where we can get down
And shout our voice, spread the message all around
For watchin out for us, and stayin aware
Inside your crib we can never be scared
Keepin it real for us and keeping it hot
Cause it don't quit and it don't stop

—D.O.

Prayers 4 Justice

Psalm 72

Give the gift of wisdom to those that rule
*   So they will be just even against the cruel*
And be there to service the low and the meek
*   Standin up for the poor, and children in need*
Come down hard on the tyrants, the ones that neglect
*   And look out for the humble, makin sure to protect*
Stand up for their beliefs, and sure to fight for this
For peace, unity and righteousness
Foes will have no choice, but to give up
*   And all enemies will bite the dust*
Even Kings and Queens will fall to their knees
*   And give it up for G-O-D*

Give the King your justice, O God,
    and your righteousness to the King's Son;
That he may rule your people righteously
    and the poor with justice;
That the mountains may bring prosperity to the people,
    and the little hills bring righteousness.
He shall defend the needy among the people;
    he shall rescue the poor and crush the oppressor.
He shall live as long as the sun and moon endure,
    from one generation to another.
He shall come down like rain upon the mown field,
    like showers that water the earth.
In his time shall the righteous flourish;
    there shall be abundance of peace till the moon shall be no more.
He shall rule from sea to sea,
    and from the River to the ends of the earth.

His foes shall bow down before him,
and his enemies lick the dust.
The kings of Tarshish and of the isles shall pay tribute,
and the kings of Arabia and Saba offer gifts.
All kings shall bow down before him,
and all the nations do him service.
For he shall deliver the poor who cries out in distress,
and the oppressed who has no helper.
He shall have pity on the lowly and poor;
he shall preserve the lives of the needy.
He shall redeem their lives from oppression and violence,
and dear shall their blood be in his sight.
Long may he live!
and may there be given to him gold from Arabia;
may prayer be made for him always,
and may they bless him all the day long.
May there be abundance of grain on the earth,
growing thick even on the hilltops;
may its fruit flourish like Lebanon,
and its grain like grass upon the earth.
May his Name remain for ever
and be established as long as the sun endures;
may all the nations bless themselves in him and
call him blessed.
Blessed be the Lord God, the God of Israel,
who alone does wondrous deeds!
And blessed be his glorious Name for ever!
and may all the earth be filled with his glory.
Amen. Amen.

AMEN. WORD!

Psalm 99

We give praise to you for all that you've done
Barely recognize what I've become
So we give it up 2 you cause you were givin it back
Walkin down the wrong trail now I see a different path
I admit that I've sinned and I paid the price
Now I've changed it around and made all that was wrong right
Thanks 4 believin in us and never giving up
Praising your name thank you for forgivin us

The Lord is King;
let the people tremble;
    he is enthroned upon the cherubim;
    let the earth shake.
The Lord is great in Zion;
    he is high above all peoples.
Let them confess his Name, which is great and awesome;
    he is the Holy One.
"O mighty King, lover of justice,
you have established equity;
    you have executed justice and righteousness in Jacob."
Proclaim the greatness of the Lord our God
and fall down before his footstool;
    he is the Holy One.
Moses and Aaron among his priests,
and Samuel among those who call upon his Name,
    they called upon the Lord, and he answered them.
He spoke to them out of the pillar of cloud;
    they kept his testimonies and the decree that he gave them.
"O Lord our God, you answered them indeed;
    you were a God who forgave them,
    yet punished them for their evil deeds."
Proclaim the greatness of the Lord our God
and worship him upon his holy hill;
    for the Lord our God is the Holy One.

Psalm 114

Yes! This is it!
When the people of God,
    friends of the Word,
House of Jacob,
    made haste outta Egypt,
the ghettos, hood of the bricks,
    they got rid of
the hater vibes,
    folks who lost grip with
what they spoke with they lips,
    like some dusty broke lyrics

They went and separated so that
    The right minds,
made the Lord's crib,
    and the Word his turf,
ripe with tight dominion.

The ocean deep,
    felt it out, n crashed about,
with all respect,
    rivers of water, the Jordan
stopped its flow,
    and headed back

the mountains bouncing around
like rams hoppin with the hills fast
and headed out,

Water, Why you gotta go,
    returning from where you're from?
Why the Jordan stop from runnin
    coming from new directions?

Why's the mountains gone act so little?
* what's the deal with hills peelin off*
instead of chillin'
* making to get away this day*
and break from what they doin'

tremble the whole world
* at the sight of the lord's movement*
at the presence of the god of jacob
* mad peace is known through it*

who flipped impossible rock,
* to raindrops*
and flint stones, into
* immaculate blooms of flowering blues,*
groups of beautiful fruit,
* riddling springs*
keepin' it fresh and new

Hallelujah!
When Israel came out of Egypt,
    the house of Jacob from a people of strange speech,
Judah became God's sanctuary
    and Israel his dominion.
The sea beheld it and fled;
    Jordan turned and went back.
The mountains skipped like rams,
    and the little hills like young sheep.
What ailed you, O sea, that you fled?
    O Jordan, that you turned back?
You mountains, that you skipped like rams?
    you little hills like young sheep?
Tremble, O earth, at the presence of the Lord,
    at the presence of the God of Jacob,
Who turned the hard rock into a pool of water
    and flint-stone into a flowing spring.

Prayer for Justice

We say a prayer for justice for equal rights
In the darkest hours, the truth will come to light
We pary to families that have been affected by violence
When theres no where to turn we ask for your guidance
We pray for those who've been wrongly convicted or accused
Our prayers go out to eh children that everyday are abused
Keep on keeping on' a new day has begun
Justice will prevail a change gon' come!

—D.O.

THE LORD IS ALL THAT

911

Clock arms passing eight, then nine
Devil arms reaching out to tear a perfect day
Human arms flapping, pouring out of windows like wine,

Thousands and thousands and thousands of voices,

Shrieking O God, O God.

—Kareem Davis

Prayers 4 Freedom

Psalm 98

Do something new for God
A new verse to spit
He's perfect: who else could give birth to this

Earth and beat down hostiles who hate him
    We dirt, yet treated like "Pop's child" salvation's
Work, but nations should praise him cause he's done it
Run'n tell a hundred people to start drum'n
Having a little fun like an aloof cartoon
    Well start smooth, dude get the flute and the harp too
Cause he's a big deal man
    We applaud the God of the Isreal Fam
Fish, Seals and marine life aquatics
    Agree that he faultless
    He gonna take office and punish the lawless.

Sing to the Lord a new song,
    for he has done marvelous things.
With his right hand and his holy arm
    has he won for himself the victory.
The Lord has made known his victory;
    his righteousness has he openly shown in the sight
    of the nations.
He remembers his mercy and faithfulness to the house of Israel,
    and all the ends of the earth have seen the victory of
    our God.
Shout with joy to the Lord, all you lands;
    lift up your voice, rejoice, and sing.
Sing to the Lord with the harp,
    with the harp and the voice of song.
With trumpets and the sound of the horn
    shout with joy before the King, the Lord.
Let the sea make a noise and all that is in it,
    the lands and those who dwell therein.
Let the rivers clap their hands,
    and let the hills ring out with joy before the Lord,
    when he comes to judge the earth.
In righteousness shall he judge the world
    and the peoples with equity.

Free At Last

Psalm 119:45

Free at last, free at last
What does it mean
to be free at last

They say you can't find freedom
By riding on a train
They say the only way to freedom
Is right on through your brain

We have freedom in the streets
And freedom in da hood
But look at the news
This freedom's no good.

Free at last, free at last
What does it mean
to be free at last

You see how can you have freedom
If you're eatin and you're drinkin
Mindin' your own business
And then your life gets taken

You have freedom to attend
The college of your choice
But with the trigger of a gun
Your freedom is destroyed

Free at last, free at last
What does it mean
to be free at last

And how can you have freedom
When you're sittin by a tree

Where they hang a noose
And then they call it liberty

You have the freedom to sit
Wherever you choose
But it's the color of the skin
That still determines the rules

Free at last, free at last
What does it mean
to be free at last

You see earth is not the place
When you're searchin for some freedom
All you need is God
'cause he's there when you need 'im

I will have an answer
For those who try to hurt me
'Cause I only speak the truth
And I know God is wit me

Free at last, free at last
Thank God Almighty
We are free at last

And I've gained perfect freedom
by following his teachin's
And I trust him so much
That I'll say it when I'm rappin'

Come say it with LOUD
   Come say it with me LOUD
We love God's commands
   We love God's commands
And we are happy now
   And we are happy now

'Cause on his promises we stand
　'Cause on his promises we stand

Free at last, free at last
Thank God Almighty
We are free at last...

—*Rap Rev Maribebop*

As I crisscross through the corridors of my complacency
I am overcome by the cries of 1,000,000 emcees.
Like ME, they too have seen the armageddon of our block,
and hurriedly scampers towards their concrete meadows,
in search of their forgotten flock
although it is said that "time waits for no man",
it seems that the big hand has tripped the little hand,
just so we could catch up.
SO AWAKEN!
All my slumbering brothas and sistas
LET NOT
this call-to-arms go unanswered
LET NOT
the repercussions of our regret
enslave us once again
like our oppressors of yester-year.

—anonymous

THAT'S WHAT'S UP

Let My People...

We pray for freedom and know what we gotta do
To get free all we have to do is follow you
All of the fighters that fight for freedom
Can't do it alone we need you to leadem'

So we pray that you can help break us out of our shakles
Cause when you got our back we can win any battle
For those being oppressed, don't give up hope
Let my people, let my people, let my people GO!

—*Brandon C. Stephens & D.O.*

Prayers 4 Peace

Psalm 15

Lord I wonder who you run with? Ride with? Be with?
I decided you abide with a V.I.P. list
Those who creep quick and steady on the tight rope
Pessimists are messy they readily back bite folk
They catch your reproach. But some are clean as soap
Beat'em til they bleed. Yes is yes, no is no
There impressive with there doe, seldom shady
Things are never non-gravy so there with you on the daily.

Lord, who may dwell in your tabernacle?
   who may abide upon your holy hill?
Whoever leads a blameless life and does what is right,
   who speaks the truth from his heart.
There is no guile upon his tongue;
he does no evil to his friend;
   he does not heap contempt upon his neighbor.
In his sight the wicked is rejected,
   but he honors those who fear the Lord.
He has sworn to do no wrong
   and does not take back his word.
He does not give his money in hope of gain,
   nor does he take a bribe against the innocent.
Whoever does these things
   shall never be overthrown.

Ecce, quam bonum + Psalm 133

How sweet is peace?
Stop'n all the drama with your fam and peeps
I bet it feels better than a man with grease
On his hair and ears fallen there and here
All on Aaron's beard
Til when he wears his gear, he can't wash it out and
I'm shout bout harmony on Hermon Mountain
And I follow the route and end up in Zion
Where Hosanna hangs out and nothing's dying.

Oh, how good and pleasant it is,
when brethren live together in unity!
It is like fine oil upon the head
that runs down upon the beard,
Upon the beard of Aaron,
and runs down upon the collar of his robe.
It is like the dew of Hermon
that falls upon the hills of Zion.
For there the Lord has ordained the blessing:
life for evermore.

SUPREME! GOD DID IT.

Let's Pray for Peace

Let's pray for peace and end to all wars
For the victims we take a moment of silence – pause
To remember that its better to look for solutions
Because there is no winning and everyone's losin'
No matter whats' happened, lets put that behind
Put an end to the beef, bring it all to a cease
Cause if we come together than we can't be beat
Put two fingers in the air and lets say PEACE

—*Brandon C. Stephens* + D.O.

When I am Mad

When I am mad and out of control,
I just don't know.
How to go to a place where
I can take it slow.

People make me mad
when they don't leave me alone.

Talking about
my business,
my family,
and my home.

Make me lose control,
makes me want to fight.

Body heats up
muscles get tight
words start flying
like windy kites.
Tail starts whipping
punching, hitting, kicking.
Try to hold me back.

—*John Anthony*

Prayers 4 The Whole of Creation

Psalm 91

If you wanna boast like "Yo' I know The Most High."
If y'all pal'around tight,
Here's what it should sound like:
Gods got my back, he's accurate at reacting
  Snatching me from the traps with promises and pacts
To injects peace, treats leave alarms gone
  He'll protect me, he's heafty, his arms, strong
So for the farm dog, the wild wolf, terror by night
  The K-9's and day time arrows in flight
For the Plagues that press past me, I'm spared the plight.
  When the thousands down dead at my left mirror my right,
I'm saved, unscathed, unfazed. None of it cometh
  Kick'n it in thicket and witness'n wicked punished
My stomach will never plummet, with fear and butterflies
  Underling run from us, it's here that God resides
They hear your every cry and the Angels respond
Through dangers and harm I remain in their arms
No pain on my palms or beneath my feet
  From rock, or beast or serpent's teeth
And the words you speak
"For those who love me
  I'll be there, when the road get ugly
Trust me, learn how I act
  Never hesitate to holla, I'll holla back
All of that is yours. Take it!
I'll come to your aid quick and give salvation"

He who dwells in the shelter of the Most High,
    abides under the shadow of the Almighty.
He shall say to the Lord,
"You are my refuge and my stronghold,
    my God in whom I put my trust."
He shall deliver you from the snare of the hunter
    and from the deadly pestilence.
He shall cover you with his pinions,
and you shall find refuge under his wings;
    his faithfulness shall be a shield and buckler.
You shall not be afraid of any terror by night,
    nor of the arrow that flies by day;
Of the plague that stalks in the darkness,
    nor of the sickness that lays waste at mid-day.
A thousand shall fall at your side
and ten thousand at your right hand,
    but it shall not come near you.
Your eyes have only to behold
    to see the reward of the wicked.
Because you have made the Lord your refuge,
    and the Most High your habitation,
There shall no evil happen to you,
    neither shall any plague come near your dwelling.
For he shall give his angels charge over you,
    to keep you in all your ways.
They shall bear you in their hands,
    lest you dash your foot against a stone.
You shall tread upon the lion and adder;
    you shall trample the young lion and the serpent under your feet.
Because he is bound to me in love,
therefore will I deliver him;
    I will protect him, because he knows my Name.
He shall call upon me, and I will answer him;
    I am with him in trouble;
    I will rescue him and bring him to honor.
With long life will I satisfy him,
    and show him my salvation.

Prayer for the Earth

God, bless the heart of Mother Earth
Bless the plant life, the water, and the dirt
Bless all the lands from the sands to the mountains
You numbered every tree, but who's counting?
Jesus, we hear you knocking
Enter the heart of the Earth and get it popping
God, bless all living things from the
Mosquitoes to the Human Beings
Thank you for the beauty of a golden sunset,
The vast oceans and the jungles unkempt
Thanks for the towns, thanks for the cities
Thank you for the gardens that are oh so pretty!
Thank you for the clouds and the air we breathe
Thank you for the trees, the leaves, and the seeds
Enter the Earth, God, make yourself known
Thank you for the Earth, our home

—*Brandon C. Stephens*

GOD IS GREAT. GOD IS GOOD.

Prayer for the World

Let us pray for the world and the children 'round the globe
For the soldiers, we pray for a safe return home
Let us all come together, every color and creed
We pray for an end to all inequalities
We pray for the planet, let us take better care of it
Let us help those in need, it doesn't matter where it is
We've got to watch the backs of all
So for the whole world, bless bless yall!

—*D.O.*

LET'S SHOW GOD SOME LOVE!

Prayer for All People Everywhere

We pray to our people every everywhere
Going thru injustice when you know it ain't fair
Even though you may be miles away
We got love for yall, that's why we pray
For the sick, the elderly, and for the children
For the nurses, doctors and parents that are with'm
All of our people that are far from home
Know that we are down for you, you are not alone!

—*Brandon C. Stephens + D.O.*

WORSHIP

RECONCILIATION
GETTING CLEAN
HOLY ANOINTING

Holy Anointing is the healing of body, mind and spirit when we become sick; when we are troubled by thoughts and actions; when our spirits confront attack and abuse; when we care for and love our families and want them to be safe and well. In Jesus Christ, we are called to Life Abundant—Life Everywhere! We also celebrate birthdays, special days and important events at Holy Anointing.

God intends for us healthy bodies, minds and souls, "To never fight or hurt anyone." From time to time, it is helpful to come to the Altar (whether alone or in public) and request Holy Anointing with the Laying-on-of-Hands by a priest or leader of the Congregation.

As in Biblical times, the holy oil is used to bless and "seal" goodness and love for the troubled, the penitent and the joyful as "Christ's Own Forever" as proclaimed at our Baptism. God is with us in deepest pain and greatest joy.

Holy Anointing

Holy Anointing takes place at "Altar Call" during Holy Eucharist (before the Confession). Individual prayers with The Reconciliation of a Penitent (The Book of Common Prayer) and Anointing are also made available.

Members of the Congregation are invited up to lay-on-hands — children and adults.

Confession is typically offered with Anointing. Prayers are extemporaneous and read, as during Altar Call, during the Holy Eucharist.

It is important to recognize that the Anointing itself becomes a sign of God's forgiveness and Love, God's safekeeping of His People and God's sharing in our happy days and celebrations!

At other times, public services of healing are offered.

A Public Service of Healing

The Gathering

The "Officiant" is the leader of Worship.

Officiant	The grace of our Lord Jesus Christ, and the love of God, and the communion of the Holy Spirit, be with you all.
People	And also with you.
Officiant	Let us pray.

After a period of silence, the Officiant says the following Collect

Loving God, the comfort of all who sorrow, the strength of all who suffer: accept our prayers, and to those who seek healing grant the power of your grace, that the weak may be strengthened, sickness turned to health, the dying made whole, and sorrow turned into joy; through Jesus Christ our Savior. Amen! *WORD!*

The Word

From the Hebrew Scriptures

A new heart I will give you, and a new spirit I will put within you; and I will remove from your body the heart of stone and give you a heart of flesh. I will put my spirit within you, and make you follow my statutes and be careful to observe my ordinances. Then you shall live in the land that I gave to your ancestors; and you shall be my people, and I will be your God.

Ezekiel 36:26-28

Psalm 103:1-5

Don't matter where you from or where you at,
He down 4 you he's got your back
Heal you and forgive your sins
Not just one or 2 but all of them
Repents you from hell, even if you a thug
He's got no grudge all he has is love!

1   Bless the LORD, O my soul,
     and all that is within me,
     bless his holy name.
2   Bless the LORD, O my soul,
     and do not forget all his benefits —
3   who forgives all your iniquity,
     who heals all your diseases,
4   who redeems your life from the Pit,
     who crowns you with steadfast love and mercy,
5   who satisfies you with good as long as you live
     so that your youth is renewed like the eagles.

From the Gospels

Come to me, all you that are weary and are carrying heavy burdens, and I will give you rest. Take my yoke upon you, and learn from me; for I am gentle and humble in heart, and you will find rest for your souls. For my yoke is easy, and my burden is light.

Matthew 11:28-30

Response to the Word

Led by the Officiant, the People are invited to make public testimony or witness to the Word.

Hip Hop Loop or Chant

The Prayers

A Litany for Healing

Officiant Let us name before God those for whom we offer our prayers.

The people offer names either silently or aloud.

Officiant Let us ask for God's healing grace by responding "Hear and have mercy"

    or "Mercy, mercy me"

    Holy God, source of health and salvation,

    Here, and after each petition, the people respond

    Hear and have mercy + Mercy, mercy me

    Holy and Mighty, wellspring of abundant life,
    Hear and have mercy + Mercy, mercy me

    Holy Immortal One, protector of the faithful,
    Hear and have mercy + Mercy, mercy me

    Holy Trinity, the source of all wholeness,
    Hear and have mercy + Mercy, mercy me

    Jesus, child of Mary, you embraced the world with your love,
    Hear and have mercy + Mercy, mercy me

Jesus, our true mother, you feed us the milk of your compassion,
Hear and have mercy + Mercy, mercy me

Jesus, eternal Christ, your promised Spirit renews our hearts and minds,
Hear and have mercy + Mercy, mercy me

Grant your grace to heal those who are sick, we pray to you, O God,
Hear and have mercy + Mercy, mercy me

Strengthen those who endure continual pain, and give them hope, we pray to you, O God,
Hear and have mercy + Mercy, mercy me

Befriend all who are anxious, lonely, or afraid, we pray to you, O God,
Hear and have mercy + Mercy, mercy me

Jesus, Lamb of God,
Hear and have mercy + Mercy, mercy me

Jesus, bearer of our sins,
Hear and have mercy + Mercy, mercy me

Jesus, redeemer of the world,
Hear and have mercy + Mercy, mercy me

The Officiant concludes the litany with this Collect
Almighty God, giver of life and health: send your blessing on all who are sick, and upon those who minister to them, that all weaknesses may be redeemed by the love of the risen Christ; who lives and reigns for ever and ever. Amen! WORD!

The Confession of Need

The Officiant says

Let us confess our need for God's healing Grace.

Silence

Each person seeking healing may move to an open healing station and give her or his name and a particular request for prayer and the laying on of hands [and anointing with oil]. The healer then lays hands upon the person [and anoints the person], prays silently, then prays aloud using the following or similar words

N., I lay my hands upon you [and anoint you]. Receive Christ's gift of healing. May the power of the Savior who suffered for you wash over you, that you may be raised up in peace and inward strength. Amen.

Officiant and People

Our Father, who art in heaven,
    hallowed be thy Name,
    thy kingdom come,
    thy will be done,
        on earth as it is in heaven.
Give us this day our daily bread.
And forgive us our trespasses,
    as we forgive those who trespass against us.
And lead us not into temptation,
    but deliver us from evil.
For thine is the kingdom, and the power, and the glory
    for ever and ever.

Amen!   Word!

The Laying on of Hands and Anointing concludes with the following Collect

Generous God, we give you thanks for your beloved Jesus Christ, in whom you have shared the beauty and pain of human life. Look with compassion upon all for whom we pray, and strengthen us to be your instruments of healing in the world, by the power of the Holy Spirit. Amen.

The priest blesses the People.

Song or Rap of Dismissal

Officiant   Let us go forth into the world, sharing God's healing grace.

People   Thanks be to God.

Adapted from Episcopal Youth Event, SERVICE OF PUBLIC HEALING

At various Seasons of the Christian Year, notably at Advent (as we pre-pare for Jesus' birth at Christmas) and Lent (as we look inward, asking God to forgive us where we have failed and to teach us His ways looking forward to Easter + Resurrection), it can be helpful to write a "Rule of Life" outlining specifically how we promise to pray, serve and worship God.

Below is an adapted form of the Nonviolent Pledge from the Southern Christian Leadership Conference used for volunteers in the American civil rights movement and for children and young people at hip hop masses.

"Rules of Life" and Pledge Certificates can be signed and blessed during Holy Eucharist at Altar with Prayers and Rap.

Children's Campaigns for Nonviolence throughout the neighborhood can be organized while inviting everyone to regularly scheduled and special Church Celebrations to promote nonviolence, peace and justice for All People.

NONVIOLENT PLEDGE

GIVING SHOUTS OUT AND BIG UPS TO THE
CHILDREN AND YOUNG PEOPLE
WHO MARCHED IN BIRMINGHAM, ALABAMA 1963-64

Adapted from The Commandments for Volunteers
Southern Christian Leadership Conference

I HEREBY PLEDGE MYSELF - MY PERSON AND BODY
TO NONVIOLENCE, PEACE AND JUSTICE
FOR ALL PEOPLE EVERYWHERE. THEREFORE I WILL
KEEP THE FOLLOWING COMMANDMENTS.

I Will

MEDITATE daily on the teachings and life of Jesus.

REMEMBER always that the nonviolent movement seeks justice
and reconciliation — not victory.

WALK AND TALK in the manner of love, for God is love.

PRAY DAILY to be used by God in order that all People
might be free.

SACRIFICE personal wishes in order that all People might be free.

OBSERVE with both friend and foe the ordinary rules of courtesy.

SEEK to perform regular service for other and for the world.

REFRAIN from violence of fist, tongue, or heart.

STRIVE to be in good spiritual and bodily health.

FOLLOW the directions of those who love and teach me.

_____

NAME, AGE AND DATE

HOLY BAPTISM

REMIX AND REBIRTH

Holy Baptism is the rite of initiation into the Church. Jesus was baptized by John the Baptist at the beginning of his earthly ministry, "In those days Jesus came from Nazareth in Galilee and was baptized by John in the Jordan." (Mark 1:9).

Holy Baptism and Holy Eucharist are the Two Great Sacraments of the Gospel ("outward and visible signs of inward and spiritual grace"). At Holy Baptism we promise to love God above all and to love our neighbors as ourselves. We celebrate these promises at every Eucharist.

We are joined at Baptism by family and 'God-family' (godparents and friends) who promise to support us in our giving and receiving of the love of God!

Those who have been

baptized in Christ,

have put on Christ.

ALLELUIA!

A Hip Hop Rite of Holy Baptism

Holy Baptism is celebrated at Holy Eucharist.

The People standing, the Celebrant says

> Blessed be the one, holy, and living God.

The MC leads the Congregation
> Glory to God for ever and ever
> *(Glory to God for ever and ever)*

The Celebrant (or Presider) continues
> There is one Body and one Spirit;

The MC leads the Congregation
> There is one hope in God's call to us;
> *(There is one hope in God's call to us)*

Celebrant
> One Lord, one Faith, one Baptism;

The MC leads the Congregation
> One God and Father of All.
> (One God and Father of All)

The MC/Rapper cries out
> Take us to the Water!

Let the People say
> Take us to the Water!
> Take us to the Water!
> Take us to the Water!

A hymn, psalm, or anthem may be sung or rapped.

A Backbeat is desirable throughout the Rite.

An MC/Rapper asks the People to stand proclaiming

HOOK + REFRAIN

**Blessed be God, Father, Son and Holy Spirit together
Forever ever, forever ever, ever ever**

Heavenly Father,
We thank you by the Holy Spirit and by the Water
Forgave your peoples of sin
Raised to a new life feeling cleansed
Give us the courage to hold us down
In your Holy Spirit hold us down
Showed us your power we recognize
To know you and love you, feel your vibe

REFRAIN + HOOK

All praise to you, we've got nuthing but love
You are great father, for raisin us up
For bringing us to this church right here
For makin us worthy so we can share
Through Jesus Christ, your Son our Lord, it's our pleasure
To show our praise. . .
Forever ever. . .

HOOK + REFRAIN

The Collect of the Day

Almighty God, by our baptism into the death and resurrection of
your Son Jesus Christ, you turn us from the old life of sin: Grant
that we, being reborn to new life in him, may live in righteousness

and holiness all our days; through Jesus Christ our Lord, who lives and reigns with you and the Holy Spirit, one God, now and for ever. Amen. *WORD!*

The Lessons

The Holy Gospel

The Sermon

The Sermon may be preached following The Peace.

Presentation and Examination of the Candidates

The Celebrant says
The Candidate(s) for Holy Baptism will now be presented.

Adults and Older Children

The candidates who are able to answer for themselves are presented individually by their Sponsors, as follows

Sponsor I present *N.* to receive the Sacrament of Baptism.

The Celebrant asks each candidate when presented
Do you desire to be baptized?
Candidate I do.

Infants and Younger Children

Then the candidates unable to answer for themselves are presented individually by their Parents and Godparents, as follows

Parents and Godparents
I present *N.* to receive the Sacrament of Baptism.

When all have been presented the Celebrant asks the parents and Godparents

Will you be responsible for seeing that the child you present is brought up in the Christian faith and life?
Parents and Godparents
I will, with God's help.

Celebrant
Will you by your prayers and witness help this child to grow into the full stature of Christ?
Parents and Godparents
I will, with God's help.

Then the Celebrant asks the following questions of the candidates who can speak for themselves, and of the parents and godparents who speak on behalf of the infants and younger children

Question	Do you renounce Satan and all the spiritual forces of wickedness that rebel against God?
Answer	I renounce them.
Question	Do you renounce the evil powers of this world which corrupt and destroy the creatures of God?
Answer	I renounce them.
Question	Do you renounce all sinful desires that draw you from the love of God?
Answer	I renounce them.
Question	Do you turn to Jesus Christ and accept him as your Savior?
Answer	I do.
Question	Do you put your whole trust in his grace and love?
Answer	I do.
Question	Do you promise to follow and obey him as your Lord?
Answer	I do.

The Baptismal Covenant

Celebrant	Do you believe in God the Father?
People	I believe in God, the Father almighty, creator of heaven and earth.

Celebrant	Do you believe in Jesus Christ, the Son of God?

People	I believe in Jesus Christ, his only Son, our Lord.
	He was conceived by the power of the Holy Spirit
	    and born of the Virgin Mary.
	He suffered under Pontius Pilate,
	    was crucified, died, and was buried.
	He descended to the dead.
	On the third day he rose again.
	He ascended into heaven,
	    and is seated at the right hand of the Father.
	He will come again to judge the living and the dead.

Celebrant	Do you believe in God the Holy Spirit?

People	I believe in the Holy Spirit,
	    the holy catholic Church,
	    the communion of saints,
	    the forgiveness of sins,
	    the resurrection of the body,
	    and the life everlasting.

Celebrant	Will you continue in the apostles' teaching and fellowship, in the breaking of bread, and in the prayers?
People	I will, with God's help.

Celebrant	Will you persevere in resisting evil, and, whenever you fall into sin, repent and return to the Lord?
People	I will, with God's help.

Celebrant	Will you proclaim by word and example, in talk and walk, the Good News of God in Christ?
People	I will, with God's help.

| Celebrant | Will you seek and serve Christ in all persons, loving your neighbor as yourself? |
| People | I will, with God's help. |

| Celebrant | Will you strive for justice and peace among all people, and respect the dignity of every human being? |
| People | I will, with God's help. |

Prayers for the Candidates

The Celebrant then says to the congregation

Let us now pray for *these persons* who *are* to receive the Sacrament of new birth.

A Person appointed leads the following petitions

| Leader | Deliver *them*, O Lord, from the way of sin and death. |
| People | Lord, hear our prayer. |

| Leader | Open *their hearts* to your grace and truth. |
| People | Lord, hear our prayer. |

| Leader | Fill *them* with your holy and life-giving Spirit. |
| People | Lord, hear our prayer. |

| Leader | Keep *them* in the faith and communion of your holy Church. |
| People | Lord, hear our prayer. |

| Leader | Teach *them* to love others in the power of the Spirit. |
| People | Lord, hear our prayer. |

| Leader | Send *them* into the world in witness to your love. |
| People | Lord, hear our prayer. |

| Leader | Bring *them* to the fullness of your peace and glory. |
| People | Lord, hear our prayer. |

The Celebrant says

Grant, O Lord, that all who are baptized into the death of Jesus Christ your Son may live in the power of his resurrection and look for him to come again in glory; who lives and reigns now and for ever. *Amen! WORD!*

Thanksgiving over the Water

The Celebrant blesses the water, first saying

The Lord be with you.
People   And also with you.

Celebrant   Let us give thanks to the Lord our God.
People   It is right to give him thanks and praise.

Celebrant

We thank you, Almighty God, for the gift of water. Over it the Holy Spirit moved in the beginning of creation. Through it you led the children of Israel out of their bondage in Egypt into the land of promise. In it your Son Jesus received the baptism of John and was anointed by the Holy Spirit as the Messiah, the Christ, to lead us, through his death and resurrection, from the bondage of sin into everlasting life. We thank you, Father, for the water of Baptism. In it we are buried with Christ in his death. By it we share in his resurrection. Through it we are reborn by the Holy Spirit. Therefore in joyful obedience to your Son, we bring into his fellowship those who come to him in faith, baptizing them in the Name of the Father, and of the Son, and of the Holy Spirit.

At the following words, the Celebrant touches the water

Now sanctify this water, we pray you, by the power of your Holy Spirit, that those who here are cleansed from sin and born again may continue for ever in the risen life of Jesus Christ our Savior.

To him, to you, and to the Holy Spirit, be all honor and glory, now and for ever. *Amen! WORD!*

Consecration of the Chrism

The Bishop may then consecrate oil of Chrism, placing a hand on the vessel of oil, and saying

Eternal Father, whose blessed Son was anointed by the Holy Spirit to be the Savior and servant of all, we pray you to consecrate this oil, that those who are sealed with it may share in the royal priesthood of Jesus Christ; who lives and reigns with you and the Holy Spirit, for ever and ever. *Amen! WORD!*

The Baptism

Each candidate is presented by name to the Celebrant, or to an assisting priest or deacon, who then immerses, or pours water upon, the candidate, saying

N., I baptize you in the Name of the Father, and of the Son, and of the Holy Spirit. *Amen! WORD!*

When desired, the people may be sprinkled with the Baptismal water as a sign of their own Baptism and the renewal of their Baptismal Covenant. During the Asperges (the blessing with water) Psalm 114 or another song may be rapped, sung or said.

Psalm 114

1   Hallelujah!
When Israel came out of Egypt,
    the house of Jacob from a people of strange speech,
2   Judah became God's sanctuary
and Israel his dominion.
3   The sea beheld it and fled;
Jordan turned and went back.
4   The mountains skipped like rams,
and the little hills like young sheep.
5   What ailed you, O sea, that you fled?

O Jordan, that you turned back?
6   You mountains, that you skipped like rams?
you little hills like young sheep?
7   Tremble, O earth, at the presence of the Lord,
at the presence of the God of Jacob.
8   Who turned the hard rock into a pool of water
and flint-stone into a flowing spring.

When this action has been completed for all candidates, the Bishop or
Priest, at a place in full sight of the congregation, prays over them, saying

Let us pray.
Heavenly Father, we thank you that by water and the Holy Spirit you
have bestowed upon *these* your *servants* the forgiveness of sin, and
have raised *them* to the new life of grace. Sustain *them*, O Lord, in
your Holy Spirit. Give *them* an inquiring and discerning heart, the
courage to will and to persevere, a spirit to know and to love you,
and the gift of joy and wonder in all your works. *Amen! WORD!*

Then the Bishop or Priest places a hand on the person's head, marking
on the forehead the sign of the cross [using Chrism if desired] and saying
to each one

N., you are sealed by the Holy Spirit in Baptism and marked as
Christ's own for ever. *Amen! WORD!*

Or this action may be done immediately after the administration of the
water and before the preceding prayer.

When all have been baptized, the Celebrant says
Let us welcome the newly baptized.

Celebrant and People
We receive you into the household of God. Confess the faith of
Christ crucified, proclaim his resurrection, and share with us in his
eternal priesthood.

An MC/Rapper leads the Congregation

B-L-E-S-S-E-D

B-l-e-s-s-e-d, what does it mean to be blessed by thee?
B-l-e-s-s-e-d, blessings are the same for you and me

If you read the Bible then you will see
That blessin's have been handed down in history

And if you keep readin you'll start believing
That you situation is not uncommon

If you've been poor or you wanted to cry
If you feel meek then you side with the weak

You see Jesus came in the same way
He came in the form of a-bay-bay

To help the persecuted and say it's ok
He suffered and he did it every day

So bless-ed are you when you get insulted
Humble yourself and you'll be exalted

For yours is the kingdom and all of it's glory
If you want to know God just keep reading the stories

The good book is written as a guide to do right
But God knows our ways, in the dark he sees light

So rejoice and be glad our reward is in heaven
Blessed in God's arms is where we'll be restin

B-l-e-s-s-e-d, day in day our
God is victory.

—*Rev. Marisol Ferrer*

The Peace is now exchanged

Celebrant   We Are One! *Amen! WORD!*
            The peace of the Lord be always with you.
People   And also with you.

The Service then continues with the Holy Eucharist.

THE BIG CELEBRATION
HOLY EUCHARIST
HOLY MATRIMONY
DEATH AND RESURRECTION

Jesus commanded us in the Gospel to remember him by coming to the table and sharing with one another in the Lord's Supper (Matthew 26:26-29; Mark 14:22-25; and, Luke 22:14-30). We confess our sins, "make clean our hearts" and prepare ourselves to receive the Lord Jesus into our lives. We come to the Table as a community of believers who, following Jesus and his disciples, then go out into the World to proclaim Christ's Love!

The Priest (the "Celebrant" or "Presider") leads the Congregation in the Celebration of Jesus' Love and victory over death on the cross. We celebrate the Resurrection of Jesus Christ at each Holy Communion. It is important that we make the Altar our home as often as possible. Holy Eucharist once weekly is a good rule. Seek out a priest or leader of the Congregation for help or conversation.

The "MC" (Master of Ceremonies) leads the People in "Call and Response" as we celebrate the Love of God for All His People!

Order of Hip Hop Mass

The Book of Common Prayer

The Holy Eucharist

*Recorded and live music begin a half-hour or more before the 'warm-up'
to welcome the People to the Celebration!*

*Simple Mass Cards (with Confession, Lord's Prayer and a psalm) may
be given to the People by ushers.*

The People are welcomed as the 'warm-up' begins.

*An MC and rapper greet the People, introducing everyone to the
tradition of "Call and Response:" "Amen! WORD!," "That's What's
Up," "Let's Show God Some Love," "God's Love Don't Stop!" and
various acclamations and responses as created and used for worship.*

A Hip Hop "Soliloquy" or Introit begins the Service.

Following the rap, the MC proclaims

> **Calling All the Rappers and Dancers of God!**
>
> **In the beginning was the Word
> and the Word was Hip Hop
> And the Word was God
> It don't quit
> And it don't stop**
>
> *or*
>
> **YO! Shout Out to All Peeps of God!
> God is in the House (Church Mass)!**
> *or*
> **God is in the Hood (Street Mass)!**

*The Church or Neighborhood Procession then begins led by 'rap
hymnody'! A Crucifer, Thurifer, Color Bearers throughout, Dancers,*

*Rappers, a Choir & All the People of God lead the way. Neighborhood
Processions are recommended for both church and street masses.*

The Word of God

The Presider then gives the Opening Acclamation with Backbeat

Blessed be the one, holy, and living God.

The MC leads the People

**And Let All the People say,
Glory to God for ever and ever.**
(Glory to God for ever and ever)

The Presider offers a prayer for the day, the Backbeat continues

Let us pray.

**Loving God, you have worked through the hearts and
minds of these your gathered people, your homies,
your brothers and sisters. Let your Word be lifted up
in the language of the streets, so that more and more
of your peeps will know You and your loving presence.
Be with us as we lift our voices in prayer and song,
giving shouts out in your name, meeting you in the
breaking of the bread. All this we ask in the name of
our Brother, our Savior, Jesus Christ. Amen! *WORD!***

A Def Word

*A reading from Holy Scripture or Holy Writing is introduced and read
with Backbeat*

*After the first reading, the same reading can be offered by second and
third readers for emphasis and learning.*

Hip Psalmody

Led by a Rapper + With Backbeat

Prayer for the Hood (for group worship)

We know the power of prayer—in our lives, in our community, in our world. With all our heart and all our mind, let us lift up the prayers of all God's people, saying Lord in your mercy, hear our prayer *take us there, take us there!*

> *Prayer Leader:* Lord in your mercy
> *People:* Lord in your mercy take us there
> *Prayer Leader:* Hear our prayer *take us there!*
> *People:* Hear our prayer *take us there!*

Let us pray for all those down with God's crew and
> For all those who recognize God's within you
> *Prayer Leader:* Lord in your mercy
> *People:* Lord in your mercy
> *Prayer Leader:* Hear our prayer *take us there!*
> *People:* Hear our prayer *take us there!*

Let us pray for the mission of the Church bringing the Hope, the Faith, the Love of Jesus to all people, for all time

> *Prayer Leader:* Lord in your mercy
> *People:* Lord in your mercy
> *Prayer Leader:* Hear our prayer *take us there!*
> *People:* Hear our prayer *take us there!*

Let us pray for this country and our leaders
> that we all may live in freedom and peace.
> You down with us, and we down with you
> cause you got the back of every and each

> *Prayer Leader:* Lord in your mercy
> *People:* Lord in your mercy
> *Prayer Leader:* Hear our prayer *take us there!*
> *People:* Hear our prayer *take us there!*

Let us pray for the world
> For good-will between nations and blessings and all peeps
> Let us holla the message cause together we can't be beat
> For peace among nations and better understanding

> *Prayer Leader*: Lord in your mercy
> *People*: Lord in your mercy
> *Prayer Leader*: Hear our prayer **take us there!**
> *People*: Hear our prayer **take us there!**

Let us pray for all those in our House, for all those in our Hood
> For all who are in prison
> For their families, and for their victims

> *Prayer Leader*: Lord in your mercy
> *People*: Lord in your mercy
> *Prayer Leader*: Hear our prayer **take us there!**
> *People*: Hear our prayer **take us there!**

Let us pray for those who have died
> For all the Founders of Hip Hop
> For the Children of Your Streets
> For the Prophets and Saints before us

> *Prayer Leader:* Lord in your mercy
> *People*: Lord in your mercy
> *Prayer Leader*: Hear our prayer **take us there!**
> *People*: Hear our prayer **take us there!**

—*Momma K (Kendra McIntosh)*

A second reading from Holy Scripture may follow the Psalm.

A Gospel Hip — rap hymnody — may precede the Holy Gospel.

The Word ✛ The Holy Gospel

The Holy Gospel is proclaimed by a Priest or Deacon, spoken or intoned with Backbeat 'loop' or 'chant' as suitable to the Gospel and Occasion.

The Sermon

With Backbeat

Altar Call

With Prayers, Holy Anointing and Holy Baptism

The Presider, MC and Rappers invite the People to Prayer. Holy Anointing and Holy Baptism are offered and celebrated as appropriated and led by the Holy Spirit. Prayers are made extemporaneously or by following the form "Prayers of the Hood" as included in "Rap, Rhyme and Prayers of the Hood."

The Confession of Sin and Absolution + With Backbeat

> **Merciful God**
> **We confess we have sinned**
> **against You and Our Neighbor.**
> **We have not done right by You.**
> **We have not done right**
> **by other People.**
> **We are sorry.**
> **We want to change.**
> **Remember Jesus, Your Son.**
> **Have mercy and forgive Us.**
> **From now on, may we try**
> **To do what You want,**
> **To the Glory of Your Name.**
>
> **Amen!** *WORD!*

The Presider offers the Absolution, the Forgiveness of Sins

> **It's cool! God forgives you ✢**
> **It's a done deal!**

The Peace

The Presider

> **Yes, Yes, Y'all**
> **The Peace of God is with You!**

MC

> **And let the people say:**
> **Yes, Yes, Y'all**
> **The Peace of God is with You!**

Following brief announcements (either here or at the conclusion of the Service), the Presider invites the People to Give to the Mission of the Church.

An Offertory Hip is offered as the Gifts of the People are made and presented.

The Holy Eucharist

The Great Thanksgiving

Backbeat throughout. The 'Sky High' Sursum Corda is led by Presider and MC

The Presider

> **May the Lord be with you, Holla Back**

MC

> **Let the People say,**
> **May the Spirit watch you and have your back**
> (May the Spirit watch you and have your back)

The Presider

> **Lift up your hearts straight to the sky**

MC

Let the People say,
We gonna lift them up to the Lord
(We gonna lift them up to the Lord)
Lift 'em up high
(Lift 'em up high)

The "Awesome Sanctus" is then led by the MC

GOD, You are Awesome
GOD, You are Awesome
GOD, You are Awesome

The whole Universe is totally filled with Your
Awesomeness
HOSANNA! ALLELUIA!

The Presider

God we praise you! Amen?

The MC leads the Congregation

WORD!
Let the People say,
We praise You, we bless You!
(we praise You, we bless You)
We represent our Love to You!
(we represent our Love to You)

The Presider

Holy God, Father, Mother of Love,
You're the One who created us;
You wanted us to work with You,
and not against You.
But we fell into sin,
We came under the power of Evil and Death.
So You sent Jesus Christ,
     Your only eternal Son.
He became a human being,

He lived and died, as one of us,
to reconcile us to You,
The God and Father of all.
For this we praise You! Amen?

The MC leads the Congregation

WORD!
Let the People say,
We praise You, we bless You!
(we praise You, we bless You)
We represent our Love to You!
(we represent our Love to You)

The Presider

Jesus stretched out His arms on the Cross,
and offered Himself as a Sacrifice for the whole World.
The night before He died for us,
Our Lord Jesus Christ took Bread:
He gave You Thanks,
He broke the Bread,
He gave it to His homies and said,
"Take this, and eat it.
This is my Body, given for you.
Do this and remember Me."
For this, God, we praise You! Amen?

The MC leads the Congregation

WORD!
Let the People say,
We praise You, we bless You!
(we praise You, we bless You)
We represent our Love to You!
(we represent our Love to You)

The Presider

Jesus took the Cup of Wine:
He gave You Thanks,
He gave it to His Homies and said,

"Drink this all of you,
This is My Blood given for you and All Peeps.
Do this and remember Me."
For this, God, we praise You! Amen?

The MC leads the Congregation

WORD!
Let the People say,
We praise You, we bless You!
(we praise You, we bless You)
We represent our Love to You!
(we represent our Love to You)

The Presider

Father, Mother God, We Celebrate
    This Memorial of our Redemption.
You save us. You love us.
You set us free.
We praise You, we bless You!
We remember Jesus' Death. Amen?   WORD!

We remember how You Raised Him
    from the Dead. Amen?   WORD!

We remember His Ascension —
    up He went into Heaven. Amen?   WORD!

God, we present to You our Gifts,
Make them Holy by Your Holy Spirit,
To be for us Your Peeps,
The Body and Blood of Jesus,
The Sacrament of New Life in Him.
For this we praise You! Amen?

The MC leads the Congregation

WORD!
Let the People say,
We praise You, we bless You!

(we praise You, we bless You)
We represent our Love to You!
(we represent our Love to You)

The Presider

> **Make US holy, at the same time.**
> **May we receive this Sacrament in total Faith.**
> > **Amen?** WORD!
> **May we serve You in unity,**
> > **always pulling together. Amen?** WORD!
> **May we serve You Forever,**
> > **never giving up. Amen?** WORD!
> **May we serve You — like Jesus — in Peace,**
> **never fighting or hurting anybody. Amen?** WORD!
> **May we be Messengers for Your Love. Amen?** WORD!
> **At the Last Day bring us,**
> > **with all Your Peeps,**
> > **with All the Founders of Hip Hop gone on,**
> > **with all the Children of Your Streets no longer here,**
> > **with Mary our Sister and All Your Saints**
> **to the joy of Your Eternal Kingdom.**
> **We ask all these things**
> **Through our Lord and Brother, Jesus Christ. Amen?**

The MC leads the Congregation

> **WORD!**
> **Let the People say,**
> **Jesus be Blessed and Praised!**
> (Jesus be Blessed and Praised)

The Presider

> **By Him, and With Him, and In Him,**
> **In the Unity of the Holy Spirit,**
> **Giving Us Life in these very moments,**
> **All Honor and Glory are Yours,**
> **Almighty Father, now and for ever.**
>
> **Amen!** **WORD!**

Amen!   WORD!
Amen!   WORD!

or

With God the Father,
For, the Son,
God, the Spirit, Three in One.

You give us life.
You give us love.
You give us blessings from above.

From the beginning of creation
To the end of the story,
All praise and honor to God's glory.
Amen!   WORD!
Amen!   WORD!
Amen!   WORD!

MC

Let us all join in hand and heart as Jesus taught us:

The Lord's Prayer

With or without Backbeat

Our Father, who art in heaven,
    hallowed be thy Name,
    thy kingdom come,
    thy will be done,
        on earth as it is in heaven.
Give us this day our daily bread.
And forgive us our trespasses,
    as we forgive those who trespass against us.
And lead us not into temptation,
    but deliver us from evil.
For thine is the kingdom, and the power, and the glory
    for ever and ever.
Amen! WORD!

The Presider breaks the Bread

The Gifts of God for all the Brothers and Sisters of God!

After a moment of silence, a Communion Hip is then begun, often with solo voice or rap slowly integrating soul, gospel and blues remix. Care is given by All to support each worshipper as Holy Communion is received.

The Postcommunion Prayer

Led by the Presider

Let us pray.
God of abundance,
You have fed us with the bread of life and cup of
    salvation;
You have united us with Christ and all our brothers
    and sisters;
and You have made us one with all Your homies and
    Your peeps in heaven and on earth.
Now send us forth into the Hood, in the power of
    Your Spirit,
that we may represent You and represent Your
    redeeming love to the world;
and continue for ever in the risen life of Christ,
    our Brother and our Savior. Amen? WORD!

✠

The Pontifical Hip Hop Blessing

God bless you and keep your back.
Amen?   WORD!

God make you a Messenger of His Love,
    at all times and to all Peeps.
Amen?   WORD!

God welcome you and yours into His Church,
    Always His Homies.
Amen?   WORD!

God bless you ✚ with peace, joy and def times forever.
Amen?   WORD!

My sistas and brothas,
All the Posse of God,
Stay Up,
Keep your head up,
Holla Back,
And go forth and tell it like it is!
    Amen!   WORD!
    Amen!   WORD!
    Amen!   WORD!

or

The Hip Hop Gospel Blessing

My Sistas and Brothas
Keep the Word at Heart!

In the beginning was the Word
And the Word was Hip Hop
And the Word was God
It Don't Quit
And It Don't Stop!

God Blesses You ✚ in His Holy Name!
    Amen!   WORD!
    Amen!   WORD!
    Amen!   WORD!

Following a hip hop 'fanfare,' the Recessional Hip is then led by the MC and Rappers as the People process into the World in celebrating the Love of GodHipHop!

Prayer 4 Marriage

We pray for these two people joining in unity
Let's give them the support of the whole community
Joined by their heart, til death due part
Such a strong bond, can't be torn apart
Even though they'll be tested it will never severe
Will only make stronger and help grow together
Thru better and worst, hand and hand
So lets pray for the marriage and for the new fam'

—*Roc & D.O.*

✠

Prayers 4 Death and Resurrection

The Magnificat Hip Hop + Luke 1: 46-55

My soul does represent the Lord,
    And my spirit has rejoiced in God my Savior and Homey.
For he has regarded
    The lowliness of his peeps.
For behold from now on
    All generations shall call me blessed.
For he that is powerful has magnified me,
    And holy is his Name, for sure.
And his mercy is on them that fear him
    Throughout all generations.
He has showed strength with his arm;
    He has scattered the proud in the imagination of their hearts.
He has dissed the mighty from their seat,
    And has uplifted the humble and meek.
He has filled the hungry with fly things,
    And the rich he has sent away empty.
Remembering his mercy, like a G, he has helped his servant Israel,
    As he promised to our forefathers and mothers,
Abraham, Sarah and their seed forever.

—*Kurtis Blow*

My soul doth magnify the Lord,
  and my spirit hath rejoiced in God my Savior.
For he hath regarded
  the lowliness of his handmaiden.
For behold from henceforth
  all generations shall call me blessed.
For he that is mighty hath magnified me,
  and holy is his Name.
And is mercy is on them that fear him
  throughout all generations.
He hath showed strength with his arm;
  he hath scattered the proud in the imagination of their hearts.
He hath put down the mighty from their seat,
  and hath exalted the humble and meek.
He hath filled the hungry with good things,
  and the rich he hath sent empty away.
He remembering his mercy hath holpen his servant Israel,
  as he promised to our forefathers,
    Abraham and his seen for ever.
Glory to the Father, and to the Son, and to the Holy Spirit;
  as it was in the beginning, is now, and will be for ever

✝

For those Who are No Longer Here

We pray for those that are no longer here...
We miss you so much, we shed tears
But you are not gone, you will live on
We will Reminisce over you as we mourn
So many leave us before their time
We know they are with you so they'll be fine
We won't forget the memories intact
We pray that you will watch over them and have their back!

—*Roc & D.O.*

Heaven

I'm loving this beautiful breeze
And enjoying the fruit from the trees
The sky changes is always something new to the scene
No need for technology
You and nature agree
But you gotta be there to see you cant take it from me
I know that heavens for free
Cause Christ paid it for me
I don't need no application
I don't need no degree
No worries no sorrows my mind always at ease

I'm going to heaven I will get there
I'm going to make it how about you

Living on earth is far more worse
Let us drink from God's well so there'll be no more thirst
There's no more sorrow
There's no more crying
There's no more thinking about Grandma dying
There's no more depression
There's no more rain
There's no more Transgressions
There's no more pain
There's no more strain
There's no more stress
There's no more games
There's no more test
There's no more working till there's no more breath

I'm going to heaven I will get there
I'm going to make it how about you

—*Missionary Men (Jahdiel Numan Puello, Eric Monk)*

Prayer for Tupac

(First delivered on the tenth anniversary of his passing, September 13, 2006)

Our Father, we thank for All Creation, especially All the Children and Young People of the World, All Roses Everywhere. We thank you for drawing children close to you and for caring for the least of these, at all times and in all places. For poet, prophet, true champion of the children and the young; friend of prisoner and outcast, marginalized and thug, we thank you for the witness, poetry and heart of Tupac Shakur. Through love and confusion, courage and failure, common to all, we thank you for Tupac's lifting up your people in prose and rhyme: For your grace, love and understanding of all humanity, O God, we shout out and celebrate Your Name which is Perfect Love for ever and ever.
AMEN! WORD!

—*Poppa T*

Thanksgivings AND BIG UPS
TO ALL THE PEOPLE OF THE FIRST HIP HOP MASSES
STREET AND ALTAR! TRINITY AVENUE AT
166TH TRINITY EPISCOPAL CHURCH OF MORRISANIA
AND THOSE WHO CONTINUE THE TRADITION
AT CHURCH OF THE ASCENSION OFF THE BOARDWALK
IN ATLANTIC CITY

WORD

Do You Not Perceive It?

Isaiah 43:16-21

Thus says the Lord, who makes a way in the sea, a path in the mighty waters, who brings out chariot and horse, army and warrior; they lie down, they cannot rise, they are extinguished, quenched like a wick: Do not remember the former things, or consider the things of old.

I am about to do a new thing; now it springs forth, do you not perceive it?

I will make a way in the wilderness and rivers in the desert. The wild animals will honour me, the jackals and the ostriches; for I give water in the wilderness, rivers in the desert, to give drink to my chosen people, the people whom I formed for myself so that they might declare my praise.

A New Thing

Isaiah 43:16-21

Forget what you've already seen…
Step back!
I'm about to do a new thing…

Open your eyes and you'll see what I mean…
Look out!
I'm about to do a new thing

Spread the word out! This is not a secret
If you can't see it, I know you must feel it
We're going to reveal it… just in case you missed it
The word remains the same - We just remixed it!

Forget about the past those dark days are done
They used to say that a change is gon' come
Well that days here! If you can't see it yet
God shows the path quicker than a GPS

Even when it look hopeless, it will all work out
Quench ya thirst, even in the desert – no doubt!
If you were looking for a sign look no more
Just be prepared for what's in store!

✠　✠　✠

Old Testament

Creation
Genesis 1:1-2:3

In the beginning when God created the heavens and the earth, the earth was a formless void and darkness covered the face of the deep, while a wind from God swept over the face of the waters. Then God said, 'Let there be light'; and there was light. And God saw that the light was good; and God separated the light from the darkness. God called the light Day, and the darkness he called Night. And there was evening and there was morning, the first day.

And God said, 'Let there be a dome in the midst of the waters, and let it separate the waters from the waters.' So God made the dome and separated the waters that were under the dome from the waters that were above the dome. And it was so. God called the dome Sky. And there was evening and there was morning, the second day.

And God said, 'Let the waters under the sky be gathered together into one place, and let the dry land appear.' And it was so. God called the dry land Earth, and the waters that were gathered together he called Seas. And God saw that it was good. Then God said, 'Let the earth put forth vegetation: plants yielding seed, and fruit trees of every kind on earth that bear fruit with the seed in it.' And it was so. The earth brought forth vegetation: plants yielding seed of every kind, and trees of every kind bearing fruit with the seed in it. And God saw that it was good. And there was evening and there was morning, the third day.

And God said, 'Let there be lights in the dome of the sky to separate the day from the night; and let them be for signs and for seasons and for days and years, and let them be lights in the dome of the sky to give light upon the earth.' And it was so. God made the two great lights—the greater light to rule the day and the lesser light to rule the night—and the stars. God set them in the dome of the sky to give light upon the earth, to rule over the day and over the night, and to separate the light from the darkness. And God saw that it was good. And there was evening and there was morning, the fourth day.

And God said, 'Let the waters bring forth swarms of living creatures, and let birds fly above the earth across the dome of the sky.' So God created the great sea monsters and every living creature that moves, of every kind, with which the waters swarm, and every winged bird of every kind. And God saw that it was good. God blessed them, saying, 'Be fruitful and multiply and fill the waters in the seas, and let birds multiply on the earth.' And there was evening and there was morning, the fifth day.

And God said, 'Let the earth bring forth living creatures of every kind: cattle and creeping things and wild animals of the earth of every kind.' And it was so. God made the wild animals of the earth of every kind, and the cattle of every kind, and everything that creeps upon the ground of every kind. And God saw that it was good.

Then God said, 'Let us make humankind in our image, according to our likeness; and let them have dominion over the fish of the sea, and over the birds of the air, and over the cattle, and over all the wild animals of the earth, and over every creeping thing that creeps upon the earth.'

So God created humankind in his image,
  in the image of God he created them;
  male and female he created them.

God blessed them, and God said to them, 'Be fruitful and multiply, and fill the earth and subdue it; and have dominion over the fish of the sea and over the birds of the air and over every living thing that moves upon the earth.' God said, 'See, I have given you every plant yielding seed that is upon the face of all the earth, and every tree with seed in its fruit; you shall have them for food. And to every beast of the earth, and to every bird of the air, and to everything that creeps on the earth, everything that has the breath of life, I have given every green plant for food.' And it was so. God saw everything that he had made, and indeed, it was very good. And there was evening and there was morning, the sixth day.

Thus the heavens and the earth were finished, and all their multitude. And on the seventh day God finished the work that he had done, and he rested on the seventh day from all the work that he had done. So God blessed the seventh day and hallowed it, because on it God rested from all the work that he had done in creation.

God's Creation

Genesis 1:1-2:3

In the beginning of the beginning
There was the word
That God spoke to bring forth
Creation of the earth
The heavens and the sky were created
God said it was good
He was pleased and elated
Created river, seas and oceans
Put life the water, set the planet in motion
And then with a wave of his hand
Brought forth vegetation, created the land
Created animals, beast,
Creatures great and small
God lives in every thing

✠　✠　✠

Our Deliverance

Exodus 14:21-15:1

Then Moses stretched out his hand over the sea. The LORD drove the sea back by a strong east wind all night, and turned the sea into dry land; and the waters were divided. The Israelites went into the sea on dry ground, the waters forming a wall for them on their right and on their left. The Egyptians pursued, and went into the sea after them, all of Pharaoh's horses, chariots, and chariot drivers. At the morning watch the LORD in the pillar of fire and cloud looked down upon the Egyptian army, and threw the Egyptian army into panic. He clogged their chariot wheels so that they turned with difficulty. The Egyptians said, 'Let us flee from the Israelites, for the LORD is fighting for them against Egypt.'

Then the LORD said to Moses, 'Stretch out your hand over the sea, so that the water may come back upon the Egyptians, upon their chariots and chariot drivers.' So Moses stretched out his hand over the sea, and at dawn the sea returned to its normal depth. As the Egyptians fled before it, the LORD tossed the Egyptians into the sea. The waters returned and covered the chariots and the chariot drivers, the entire army of Pharaoh that had followed them into the sea; not one of them remained. But the Israelites walked on dry ground through the sea, the waters forming a wall for them on their right and on their left.

Thus the LORD saved Israel that day from the Egyptians; and Israel saw the Egyptians dead on the seashore. Israel saw the great work that the LORD did against the Egyptians. So the people feared the LORD and believed in the LORD and in his servant Moses.

Then Moses and the Israelites sang this song to the LORD:
'I will sing to the LORD, for he has triumphed gloriously;
horse and rider he has thrown into the sea.

God Is Freedom

Exodus 14:21-15:1

Deliver Us from Evil, God's Power and his Glory
Delivering his people, God's Power and his Glory
Follow and He will lead you, God's Power and his Glory
Believe and he will guide you, God's Power and his Glory

Moses led Israel out of bondage,
But the people still feared
No food in the wilderness
"We might die out there"
God said to Moses, "lift your staff
Go through the sea
When I split it in half."
The pharaoh and his army followed
Egypt's people in chariots
Pursued the Israelites with a fury
But God was in the midst
A cloud appeared in the sky that God formed
A storm followed.
Then Egypt's army saw God's power
They were quite startled
No longer wanted conflict
They attempted to flee
Moses stretched his hand
And the Army drowned in the sea
God saved Israel

Follow and He will lead you, God's Power and his Glory
Believe and he will guide you, God's Power and his Glory

✠ ✠ ✠

Ruth and Naomi

Ruth 1:11-22

But Naomi said, 'Turn back, my daughters, why will you go with
me? ...Then they wept aloud again. Orpah kissed her mother-in-law,
but Ruth clung to her.

So she said, 'See, your sister-in-law has gone back to her people and
to her gods; return after your sister-in-law.' But Ruth said,

'Do not press me to leave you
    or to turn back from following you!
Where you go, I will go;
    where you lodge, I will lodge;
your people shall be my people,
    and your God my God.
Where you die, I will die—
    there will I be buried.
May the LORD do thus and so to me,
    and more as well,
if even death parts me from you!'
When Naomi saw that she was determined to go with her, she said
    no more to her.
So the two of them went on until they came to Bethlehem. When
    they came to Bethlehem, the whole town was stirred because of
    them; and the women said, 'Is this Naomi?' She said to them,

'Call me no longer Naomi,
    call me Mara,
    for the Almighty has dealt bitterly with me.
I went away full,
    but the LORD has brought me back empty;
why call me Naomi
    when the LORD has dealt harshly with me,
    and the Almighty has brought calamity upon me?'
So Naomi returned together with Ruth the Moabite, her daughter-
    in-law, who came back with her from the country of Moab.
    They came to Bethlehem at the beginning of the barley harvest.

Friendship

Ruth 1:11-22

Don't call me my name, you can call me bitter
Road getting rough, Lord please forgive us
Haven't given up yet, don't call me a quitter
My soul, runs deep like rivers

You can tell me to leave, but I won't go
You know I'm down and I got ya back fa sho
Whether you feeling high, or down low
I'ma hold you down, this you should know
Yeah I know, its been hard life hasn't been fair
When it comes to problems, you've had more than your share
Don't know when its goin to come and from where
When it all falls down, how do you prepare?
Will not leave you, stick by your side
Stand tall with you, will not hide
Whenever, Where ever, I'm down to ride
We goin make it thru, goin be alright
Nothin going come between us, we too strong
Can't break us, we're going to carry on
Stay driven even though the road seems so long
We goin keep goin... on and on and on and on

✠ ✠ ✠

A Great Prophet

Amos 5:14-15; 21-24

Seek good and not evil,
  that you may live;
and so the LORD, the God of hosts, will be with you,
  just as you have said.
Hate evil and love good,
  and establish justice in the gate;
it may be that the LORD, the God of hosts,
  will be gracious to the remnant of Joseph.

I hate, I despise your festivals,
  and I take no delight in your solemn assemblies.
Even though you offer me your burnt-offerings and grain-offerings,
  I will not accept them;
and the offerings of well-being of your fatted animals
  I will not look upon.
Take away from me the noise of your songs;
  I will not listen to the melody of your harps.
But let justice roll down like waters,
  and righteousness like an ever-flowing stream.

LET JUSTICE
LIKE
WATER

God Is Justice

Amos 5:14-15; 21-24

Will you stay on the road through the good
    and bad times...
Are you down to ride?
Will you stand up or will you hide?
Are you down to ride?

I know it looks so good... looks so great and
You want it at right now, no time to wait
All at once, forget moderation
What will you choose? So much temptation?

Give a hand to ya man, that's your brother
Lord knows, watching us from above
Cause in the end there will be justice!
We just need to hold onto the love

Its more than what you put in ya offerein plate...
Gotta look at yourself and watch what you say...
Cause God don't care bout ya fancy parties...

Give a hand to ya man, that's your brother
Lord knows, watching us from above
We just need to hold onto the love
Cause in the end there will be justice!

✠ ✠ ✠

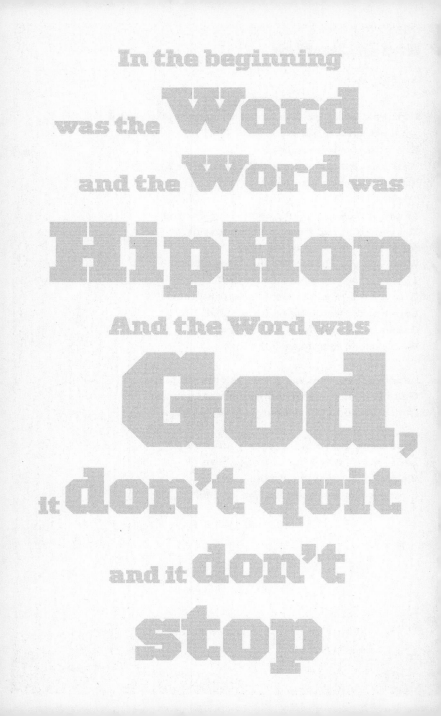

New Testament

Incarnation

John 1:1-14

In the beginning was the Word, and the Word was with God, and the Word was God. He was in the beginning with God. All things came into being through him, and without him not one thing came into being. What has come into being in him was life, and the life was the light of all people. The light shines in the darkness, and the darkness did not overcome it.

There was a man sent from God, whose name was John. He came as a witness to testify to the light, so that all might believe through him. He himself was not the light, but he came to testify to the light. The true light, which enlightens everyone, was coming into the world.

He was in the world, and the world came into being through him; yet the world did not know him. He came to what was his own, and his own people did not accept him. But to all who received him, who believed in his name, he gave power to become children of God, who were born, not of blood or of the will of the flesh or of the will of man, but of God.

And the Word became flesh and lived among us, and we have seen his glory, the glory as of a father's only son, full of grace and truth.

God Is Everywhere

John 1:1-14

Couldn't express the feeling I was looking for the words
My man on the block came up and said "word!"
Tossin and turnin like I couldn't sleep
And when I woke up, looked up to see
The word was flesh and dwelt in the hood
And when the sun rose it was all understood
That all I had to do was think it, cause if I speak it,
I can be it… and live all my dreams
I was lookin all over, couldn't find a clue
Till I realized, it's in me, it's in you
Said I was lookin all over, searchin for the truth
Till I realized, it's in me, it's in you

The word was flesh and dwelt in the hood
And when the sun rose it was all understood

John the Baptist

Mark 1:1-8

The beginning of the good news of Jesus Christ, the Son of God.

As it is written in the prophet Isaiah,
'See, I am sending my messenger ahead of you,
  who will prepare your way;
the voice of one crying out in the wilderness:
  "Prepare the way of the Lord,
  make his paths straight",'

John the baptizer appeared in the wilderness, proclaiming a baptism of repentance for the forgiveness of sins. And people from the whole Judean countryside and all the people of Jerusalem were going out to him, and were baptized by him in the river Jordan, confessing their sins. Now John was clothed with camel's hair, with a leather belt around his waist, and he ate locusts and wild honey. He proclaimed, 'The one who is more powerful than I is coming after me; I am not worthy to stoop down and untie the thong of his sandals. I have baptized you with water; but he will baptize you with the Holy Spirit.'

Holy Baptism

Mark 1:1-8

Down at the river was a man named John,
Change your life around, no matter what's gone wrong
John was not "the" one, but he held the key
Behind the scenes was G-O-D

Only one thing that's got to be done
Give up your old life, for the kingdom!
Down by the river, for the baptism
Came back different, came back livin!

The road was so hard so many bumps and holes
Now it was all clear, set to go
Livin in despair, times of doubt
Holy spirit made the change from the inside out!

✠ ✠ ✠

Mary, Our Mother

Luke 1:46-55

And Mary said,
'My soul magnifies the Lord,
  and my spirit rejoices in God my Saviour,
for he has looked with favour on the lowliness of his servant.
  Surely, from now on all generations will call me blessed;
for the Mighty One has done great things for me,
  and holy is his name.
His mercy is for those who fear him
  from generation to generation.
He has shown strength with his arm;
  he has scattered the proud in the thoughts of their hearts.
He has brought down the powerful from their thrones,
  and lifted up the lowly;
he has filled the hungry with good things,
  and sent the rich away empty.
He has helped his servant Israel,
  in remembrance of his mercy,
according to the promise he made to our ancestors,
  to Abraham and to his descendants for ever.'

Our Partnership with God

Luke 1:46-55

The mighty one she's done great things for me
Just look around and you can see... The mighty one
she's done great things for me
So I holla her name out in the streets...

The mighty one's done great things for me...
I followed the Word and it set me free
Comin from the streets where I wasn't given nuthin
Mighty one blessed me, didn't see it comin

Stayed humble even when times were not good
Through the darkness when many were shook
That's because G-O-D is so magnificent
So magnificent... you gotta get wit it!

Don't need to have paper, to feel the power
Got your back, every minute, every hour
Rollin thru this way and comin thru hard
Representin for the underdog!

Got this feelin, can feel it in my soul
Bout to change the game like you'd never know!
That's because G-O-D is so magnificent
So magnificent... you gotta get wit it!

✠ ✠ ✠

Jesus Is Born!

Luke 2:1-20

In those days a decree went out from Emperor Augustus that all the world should be registered. This was the first registration and was taken while Quirinius was governor of Syria. All went to their own towns to be registered. Joseph also went from the town of Nazareth in Galilee to Judea, to the city of David called Bethlehem, because he was descended from the house and family of David. He went to be registered with Mary, to whom he was engaged and who was expecting a child. While they were there, the time came for her to deliver her child. And she gave birth to her firstborn son and wrapped him in bands of cloth, and laid him in a manger, because there was no place for them in the inn.

In that region there were shepherds living in the fields, keeping watch over their flock by night. Then an angel of the Lord stood before them, and the glory of the Lord shone around them, and they were terrified. But the angel said to them, 'Do not be afraid; for see— I am bringing you good news of great joy for all the people: to you is born this day in the city of David a Savior, who is the Messiah, the Lord. This will be a sign for you: you will find a child wrapped in bands of cloth and lying in a manger.' And suddenly there was with the angel a multitude of the heavenly host, praising God and saying,

'Glory to God in the highest heaven,
and on earth peace among those whom he favors!'

When the angels had left them and gone into heaven, the shepherds said to one another, 'Let us go now to Bethlehem and see this thing that has taken place, which the Lord has made known to us.' So they went with haste and found Mary and Joseph, and the child lying in the manger. When they saw this, they made known what had been told them about this child; and all who heard it were amazed at what the shepherds told them. But Mary treasured all these words and pondered them in her heart. The shepherds returned, glorifying and praising God for all they had heard and seen, as it had been told them.

Love Is Victor!

Luke 2:1-20

We goin set it off tonight we going celebrate
We goin party tonight cause its his birthday!
They comin from all over, from far away
Sold out and couldn't find a place to stay
The son of God still couldn't find a room
Born in the slums without a silver spoon
Soon as they heard the word, that's when they came
Left knowin they'd never be the same again
They couldn't imagine if they tried
Couldn't believe till they saw with their own two eyes
The angel was right she was keeping it real
It was too much, couldn't describe how they feel
Who would have thought they'd find the savior
Not in a royal crib but chillin in a manager
So Bless the lord for this little boy
Spread the word to the world, bringing so much joy!

✠ ✠ ✠

Feeding of 5000

John 6:1-15

After this Jesus went to the other side of the Sea of Galilee, also called the Sea of Tiberias. A large crowd kept following him, because they saw the signs that he was doing for the sick. Jesus went up the mountain and sat down there with his disciples. Now the Passover, the festival of the Jews, was near. When he looked up and saw a large crowd coming towards him, Jesus said to Philip, 'Where are we to buy bread for these people to eat?' He said this to test him, for he himself knew what he was going to do. Philip answered him, 'Six months' wages would not buy enough bread for each of them to get a little.' One of his disciples, Andrew, Simon Peter's brother, said to him, 'There is a boy here who has five barley loaves and two fish. But what are they among so many people?' Jesus said, 'Make the people sit down.' Now there was a great deal of grass in the place; so they sat down, about five thousand in all. Then Jesus took the loaves, and when he had given thanks, he distributed them to those who were seated; so also the fish, as much as they wanted. When they were satisfied, he told his disciples, 'Gather up the fragments left over, so that nothing may be lost.' So they gathered them up, and from the fragments of the five barley loaves, left by those who had eaten, they filled twelve baskets. When the people saw the sign that he had done, they began to say, 'This is indeed the prophet who is to come into the world.'

When Jesus realized that they were about to come and take him by force to make him king, he withdrew again to the mountain by himself.

All Are Fed!

John 6:1-15

Everyone was chillin, having a good time
Jesus took a look out saw the crowd arrive

We all gotta eat
We're about to have a feast
Not enough fish,
Not enough bread
But Jesus had another plan instead
Came up with a way for them all to get fed

All of a sudden, food was ready
Couldn't believe their eyes but felt it in their bellys
Everyone got enough, filled their plate
Gathered leftovers so nothing went to waste

Before they weren't convinced, they used to gossip
But now they realized, this is the prophet!

✠ ✠ ✠

The Way of the Cross

Matthew 27:1-54

When morning came, all the chief priests and the elders of the people conferred together against Jesus in order to bring about his death. They bound him, led him away, and handed him over to Pilate the governor.

When Judas, his betrayer, saw that Jesus was condemned, he repented and brought back the thirty pieces of silver to the chief priests and the elders. He said, 'I have sinned by betraying innocent blood.' But they said, 'What is that to us? See to it yourself.' Throwing down the pieces of silver in the temple, he departed; and he went and hanged himself. But the chief priests, taking the pieces of silver, said, 'It is not lawful to put them into the treasury, since they are blood money.' After conferring together, they used them to buy the potter's field as a place to bury foreigners. For this reason that field has been called the Field of Blood to this day. Then was fulfilled what had been spoken through the prophet Jeremiah, 'And they took the thirty pieces of silver, the price of the one on whom a price had been set, on whom some of the people of Israel had set a price, and they gave them for the potter's field, as the Lord commanded me.'

Now Jesus stood before the governor; and the governor asked him, 'Are you the King of the Jews?' Jesus said, 'You say so.' But when he was accused by the chief priests and elders, he did not answer. Then Pilate said to him, 'Do you not hear how many accusations they make against you?' But he gave him no answer, not even to a single charge, so that the governor was greatly amazed.

Now at the festival the governor was accustomed to release a prisoner for the crowd, anyone whom they wanted. At that time they had a notorious prisoner, called Jesus Barabbas. So after they had gathered, Pilate said to them, 'Whom do you want me to release for you, Jesus Barabbas or Jesus who is called the Messiah?' For he realized that it was out of jealousy that they had handed him over. While he was sitting on the judgement seat, his wife sent word to him, 'Have nothing to do with that innocent man, for today I have suffered a great deal because of a dream about him.' Now the chief priests and the elders persuaded the crowds to ask for Barabbas and to have Jesus killed. The governor again said to them, 'Which of the two do you want me to release for you?' And they said, 'Barabbas.' Pilate said to them, 'Then what should I do with Jesus who is called the Messiah?' All of them said, 'Let him be crucified!' Then he asked, 'Why, what evil has he done?' But they shouted all the more, 'Let him be crucified!'

So when Pilate saw that he could do nothing, but rather that a riot was beginning, he took some water and washed his hands before the crowd, saying, 'I am innocent of this man's blood; see to it yourselves.' Then the people as a whole answered, 'His blood be on us and on our children!' So he released Barabbas for them; and after flogging Jesus, he handed him over to be crucified.

Then the soldiers of the governor took Jesus into the governor's headquarters, and they gathered the whole cohort around him. They stripped him and put a scarlet robe on him, and after twisting some thorns into a crown, they put it on his head. They put a reed in his right hand and knelt before him and mocked him, saying, 'Hail, King of the Jews!' They spat on him, and took the reed and struck him on the head. After mocking him, they stripped him of the robe and put his own clothes on him. Then they led him away to crucify him.

As they went out, they came upon a man from Cyrene named Simon; they compelled this man to carry his cross. And when they came to a place called Golgotha (which means Place of a Skull), they offered him wine to drink, mixed with gall; but when he tasted it, he would not drink it. And when they had crucified him, they divided his clothes among themselves by casting lots; then they sat down there and kept watch over him. Over his head they put the charge against him, which read, 'This is Jesus, the King of the Jews.'

Then two bandits were crucified with him, one on his right and one on his left. Those who passed by derided him, shaking their heads and saying, 'You who would destroy the temple and build it in three days, save yourself! If you are the Son of God, come down from the cross.' In the same way the chief priests also, along with the scribes and elders, were mocking him, saying, 'He saved others; he cannot save himself. He is the King of Israel; let him come down from the cross now, and we will believe in him. He trusts in God; let God deliver him now, if he wants to; for he said, "I am God's Son." ' The bandits who were crucified with him also taunted him in the same way.

From noon on, darkness came over the whole land until three in the afternoon. And about three o'clock Jesus cried with a loud voice, 'Eli, Eli, lema sabachthani?' that is, 'My God, my God, why have you forsaken me?' When some of the bystanders heard it, they said, 'This man is calling for Elijah.' At once one of them ran and got a sponge, filled it with sour wine, put it on a stick, and gave it to him to drink. But the others said, 'Wait, let us see whether Elijah will come to save him.' Then Jesus cried again with a loud voice and breathed his last. At that moment the curtain of the temple was torn in two, from top to bottom. The earth shook, and the rocks were split. The tombs also were opened, and many bodies of the saints who had fallen asleep were raised. After his resurrection they came out of the tombs and entered the holy city and appeared to many. Now when the centurion and those with him, who were keeping watch over Jesus, saw the earthquake and what took place, they were terrified and said, 'Truly this man was God's Son!'

I Am

Jesus' Life for Us

Matthew 27:1-54

Could have done anything but he gave it up
Just so that he could give his Life for Us...
Could have been anything but he gave it up
So that he could give his Life for Us...

At the first light of dawn, they finished their plan
They were out to prove that he was just a man
Judas knew he was doomed
And the plan was about to go down soon

In court, front of the town
Even when faced with the threat of violence
Kept his lips sealed, he chose silence

They spit on him, nailed him to a cross
But his movement would not stop!
There was an earthquake that shook the ground
Tombs opened up from all around!

Realized that their work was not done
That's when they knew that it had to be the Son

✠ ✠ ✠

God's Son

Easter + Resurrection

Matthew 28:1-10

After the sabbath, as the first day of the week was dawning, Mary Magdalene and the other Mary went to see the tomb. And suddenly there was a great earthquake; for an angel of the Lord, descending from heaven, came and rolled back the stone and sat on it. His appearance was like lightning, and his clothing white as snow. For fear of him the guards shook and became like dead men. But the angel said to the women, 'Do not be afraid; I know that you are looking for Jesus who was crucified. He is not here; for he has been raised, as he said. Come, see the place where he lay. Then go quickly and tell his disciples, "He has been raised from the dead, and indeed he is going ahead of you to Galilee; there you will see him." This is my message for you.' So they left the tomb quickly with fear and great joy, and ran to tell his disciples. Suddenly Jesus met them and said, 'Greetings!' And they came to him, took hold of his feet, and worshipped him. Then Jesus said to them, 'Do not be afraid; go and tell my brothers to go to Galilee; there they will see me.'

Christ Is Back!

Matthew 28:1-10

Refrain
Leader: Spread the word out, there's no doubt...
People: CHRIST IS BACK!
Leader: Alleuluia, couldn't have come sooner
People: CHRIST IS BACK!
Tried 2 pull the wool ova our eyes
Can't stop us we gon' rise...
Enuff's enuff.... we callin they bluff...
G-O-D, rollin wit us...
That's why we celebrate
She saw visions, didn't hallucinate
I'm tell in you, please believe
Christ is back on the scene...
It's for real!
It was the truth at the cemetery. . .
Rubbed her eyes, but still Mary,
Knew what she saw alright...
The return of Jesus Christ!
Refrain
Got me excited, feelin so eager...
Christ has risen, today on Easter
Saw the vision, stayed on the mission
Best belive, Christ is risen
To think, it was just the other day...
Head hung down low on Friday. ..
Now the whole world can see...
Thank you G-O-D
Can't hold in what we saw, made the confession
Christ is back! It's the Resurrection
That's why we sing the spiritual
Nothing less than a miracle
Refrain

✠   ✠   ✠

Pentecost

Acts 2:1-11

When the day of Pentecost had come, they were all together in one place. And suddenly from heaven there came a sound like the rush of a violent wind, and it filled the entire house where they were sitting. Divided tongues, as of fire, appeared among them, and a tongue rested on each of them. All of them were filled with the Holy Spirit and began to speak in other languages, as the Spirit gave them ability.

Now there were devout Jews from every nation under heaven living in Jerusalem. And at this sound the crowd gathered and was bewildered, because each one heard them speaking in the native language of each. Amazed and astonished, they asked, 'Are not all these who are speaking Galileans? And how is it that we hear, each of us, in our own native language? Parthians, Medes, Elamites, and residents of Mesopotamia, Judea and Cappadocia, Pontus and Asia, Phrygia and Pamphylia, Egypt and the parts of Libya belonging to Cyrene, and visitors from Rome, both Jews and proselytes, Cretans and Arabs—in our own languages we hear them speaking about God's deeds of power.'

Holy Spirit Power

Acts 2:1-11

One mic, one life, one love
One God, in the Heavens Above
You'll feel it when you see it
Know it when you hear it
That's the Power of the Holy Spirit!

They were all chillin before it was set to begin
Then they heard a sound like a strong wind
Came from the ground went higher and higher
Spread through the place like a wild fire

All came together from different places
Different classes, cultures, different races
All had different words, different slang
So different yet so much the same!

Then something happened, no one could explain
Thought it was a trick, some sort of game
There was only one language, one way to speak
Everybody could understand each

Some people to the side didn't know what to think
Figured it was something in the wine that they drink!
That's when they knew the Word came from above
One Mic, One Life, One God, One Love!

✠ ✠ ✠

God With Us

Revelation 21:1-7

Then I saw a new heaven and a new earth; for the first heaven and the first earth had passed away, and the sea was no more. And I saw the holy city, the new Jerusalem, coming down out of heaven from God, prepared as a bride adorned for her husband. And I heard a loud voice from the throne saying,

'See, the home of God is among mortals.
He will dwell with them;
they will be his peoples,
and God himself will be with them;
he will wipe every tear from their eyes.
Death will be no more;
mourning and crying and pain will be no more,
for the first things have passed away.'

And the one who was seated on the throne said, 'See, I am making all things new.' Also he said, 'Write this, for these words are trustworthy and true.' Then he said to me, 'It is done! I am the Alpha and the Omega, the beginning and the end. To the thirsty I will give water as a gift from the spring of the water of life. Those who conquer will inherit these things, and I will be their God and they will be my children.

God's Children Forever

Revelation 21:1-7

New Heaven, New Earth, The old was gone
The Holy City New Jerusalem God had formed
There was a voice from the throne,
The home of God amongst his people
In God's love we all are equal
Making all things brand new
Words that ring true
These words I say to you & you & you & you
Hear these words, write these words
"I am the Alpha & Omega,
I rule as Lord over my children,
They will be with me For ever
 I rule as Lord over my people
They will be with me For ever
 I rule as Lord over my children,
They will be with me For ever

✠ ✠ ✠

BACKUP

Hip Hop Gospel

By The Reverend Lynne Washington
Missioner for Outreach
The Diocese of Virginia

> Black rap music is primarily the musical expression of the paradox-
> ical cry of desperation and celebration of the black underclass and
> poor working class, a cry that openly acknowledges and confronts
> the wave of personal coldheartedness, criminal cruelty and existen-
> tial hopelessness in the black ghettos of Afro-America... Black rap
> music is the last form of transcendence available to young black
> ghetto dwellers.
> —Cornell West, *On Afro-American Music: From Bebob to Rap*, 1982

THEOLOGY IS A CONVERSATION about God, a conversation with God,
a conversation for God. Theology is God talk and is about the ways and
knowledge of God. It is God's language about an aspect of human life. Hip
hop is theological language. Hip hop is a community opening itself to a
prophetic "Word" from God. The Word stirred from the depths of the chaot-
ic beginnings of creation, when little good was initially seen in the darkness
(Genesis 1:1-5). In the beginning, little good was expected from hip hop, but
God can make all things new! In the act of creation God later revealed the
beauty of life in all its aspects and the design of humanity with a plan and
purpose (Genesis 1:26-27). God's grace entered into this experience and once
again God called it good (Genesis 1:31). **Hip hop as was birthed from the well
of liberation theology, more specifically, the black theological experiences of
urban youth.**

The largest generation of African American entrepreneurs is associated
with the hip hop genre. This generation has the potential for becoming, if it
isn't already, the wealthiest generation of Blacks in history. "At its best, hip
hop is an unmatched vehicle for influence and change. At its worst, the culture can mire an entire generation in commercialism and misogyny," stated
hip hop commentator, Jerry L. Barrow. This liberation is from the freedom
that comes with economic opportunities, something most African
Americans knew nothing about, having existed in a society that has consis-
tently dismissed their humanity, intellect and perseverance. This freedom
only comes from the crucifixion-like experience of knowing the suffering

that comes from being different and speaking honestly about the evils that plague our society. **If one believes that Jesus came to relieve the poor and suffering, then one must also believe that Jesus speaks through Hip Hop Gospel, which ministers in poor and struggling communities.**

Hip hop has evolved into storytelling, that is, in the telling of a story that begins in confusion but becomes life-giving to many. **The voice of hip hop cries out in the wilderness for salvation, cries out to be saved from a world that sustains the "human food chain": the prison industrial complex, corporate greed, unequal educational opportunities, and violence—these are systems that have left behind the least amongst us (Isaiah 61:1, 2; 58:6).** Hip hop is consistent with the black struggle for justice. This is in contrast to the growth in the evangelical movement in Christianity and its greater emphasis on obedience and discipline. The theology of liberation states that God will relieve the suffering of His people from the oppressive nature of colonialism and white supremacy, and that heaven is not a transcendent thing that exists to divert African Americans from the realities of their everyday lives.

Hip Hop Gospel rejects the notion that God only speaks to other Christians through the music of Handel, Bach, and even what is thought of as contemporary Christian praise music. Instead, Hip Hop Gospel puts God on the street corner along with boom boxes, low riders, and even MP3 players. It pushes against the limits of classism and elitism in Christian worship experience and practice. The music of Gospel Hip Hop teaches that one can be young, gifted, black and in the streets proclaiming Christ; one's personal situation cannot keep one from Christ (Mark 9:42-43; 10:15-16). Hip hop takes us out of the traditional liturgical settings in big cathedrals and institutional churches to the streets of hard knocks, which are open to the Good News of Christ. The voice of Jesus loudly calls out to those that we tend to run from in order to protect our wallets and purses. **Hip hop is the fervor and power of the streets based in Jesus Christ! (Mark 9:1).**

Hip hop is not embraced by those outside the walls of the institution we call "the church". It is not embraced in hymnals nor in the Anglican tradition. Remember that the prophetic voice of the streets can touch us as Jesus touched the Pharisees and Sadducees with truth. The religious faithful of our time deem Gospel Hip Hop guilty by association; to them, the voices of this genre cannot be holy because everything traditionally associated with hip hop has not been approved by the religious establishment of our time as sanctified by God . **The same act of the Spirit that transformed Gospel from the music of the brothels and speakeasies, music that once had seemingly no redeeming value, is the same Spirit that has taken hip hop to the mountain top for its transformation into the next, greatest evangelism tool.**

In the Beginning – WORD!

A Reflection on Liturgical Theology.

The Reverend Peter F. Grandell

"In the beginning was the Word . . ." John 1:1

IN THE OPENING WORDS of the great Prologue to the Gospel of John, the Evangelist makes us witnesses to a "new thing". The cadences and rhythms of the familiar words live comfortably in our ears and hearts. These words are meaningful—that is, full of signification, symbol and memory. They carry with them a multiplicity of meaning. They carry with them the meaning of the Christian community, which has endured over centuries (in this case, it is the glory of God coming to dwell with us in the full person and being of Jesus Christ). They also carry with them the meaning that we ourselves bring to them (as we recall hearing these words on Christmas Day and remembering what the church looked like, the dinner that was served that afternoon, and who was with us at the time). Finally, hidden deep within these words is a meaning that has yet to be found and remembered by future generations of those who will hear and believe. The writer of this Gospel purposefully echoed the very first words of the Hebrew Scriptures (Genesis 1:1)—"In the beginning . . . ;" a set of words that originally harkened to the acts of the Creator alone. **But these words were broken open, if you will, to include the new reality and understanding of God incarnate, dead and risen in Jesus Christ.** In "breaking," the old had been used to explain and understand the new; and in the power of the Spirit, God's "new thing" has been given voice.

Our liturgies are alive with "broken words," as liturgical scholar Gordon Lathrop calls them. (*Holy Things, A Liturgical Theology*, Augsburg Fortress Publishers, 1995.) The Passover of the Hebrews has become "Christ our Passover." The Hebrews' Exodus from Egypt has become our exodus from death to life. The Passover lamb has become Angus Dei, the Lamb of God, the sacrificial offering that ended all human sacrifice; the once and for all offering on Calvary. Time and again we Christians have looked to our past to make sense of our present. (A present understood in light of God's salvific work in Christ and the Reign of God that Christ heralded.) The Church has taken that which it has known and loved and reshaped and renamed it to include the "new creation" that we now see and understand as Christ continues to "live and move" among us "in spirit and in truth" in that great, **ever unfolding Kingdom.**

This process of breaking open our old symbol sets and systems is ongoing. This process was alive not just for the earliest of believers, but is alive and well for us today. **In the HipHopEMass, we see these broken words take on new, fresh meaning and, more importantly, immediacy.** We all know the words of the 23rd Psalm; they too are familiar and rhythmic in our hearts and ears. "Yea, though I walk through the valley of the shadow of death, I will fear no evil; for thou art with me; thy rod and thy staff, they comfort me." Listening to these words, images of the Good Shepherd abound; crooks and staffs flit through our memories. We love the metaphor of the journey. Death has become distanced for us, reduced to a shadow. This Psalm is lovely, meaningful, and important, but something has been lost. We no longer have access to the immediacy of need and absolute dependence on God that the psalmist was trying to communicate, that dependency and need of God that we have in the face of real and tangible danger. Back in the day of the psalmist, to be alone with the sheep amongst the wolves of the desert was to court real danger, and the threats of flash floods, robbery and even death were harsh realities, if not certainties. **HipHopEMass has reclaimed this immediacy for us.**

Arising out the context of New York City's South Bronx, we now hear these words: "And even though I walk through the Hood of death, I don't back down for you have my back." Walking through the [neighbor]hood of death is a harsh, gritty reality for many of us on the back streets of the stark urban landscape of the inner city. Just leaving our front doors and stepping out onto our stoops can put us in harm's way. Street fights, muggings, rapes, drive-by shootings—the list goes on—are everyday realities in our poorest and most violent neighborhoods. Innocent lives that are in harm's way everyday, with no means of escape, can testify to the presence of the "Word made Flesh" upon whom our survival depends, and who holds us in the bosom of absolute Love. Words are real, stark, and meaningful. **New words can break open old realities and truths and help us to apprehend, in ever-widening ways, the immediacy of God for us and with us.**

> "And the Word was made flesh and lived among us,
> and we have seen his glory,
> the glory as of a father's only son,
> full of grace and truth."
> (John 1:14)

Far from being an "innovation," the HipHopEMass is rooted in the earliest of Christian traditions, traditions which it honors and uses toward the strengthening of the reign of God. May all who pray with these words be filled by God's spirit; refreshed by the love of Christ; and emboldened to proclaim the truth of God's reign—here and now. **Amen! Word!**

Evangelism

From DJ Cool Clyde

WHAT'S UP, I'M DJ Cool Clyde, Hip Hop Pioneer from the Boogie Down Bronx—The 1st DJ to Scratch on Wax (records) Worldwide.

I give my props 2 the Most High and Jesus Christ for allowing me to know and understand my purpose here on earth.

My mission is to bridge the gap between the young and the mature of all ethnicities, races, colors, creeds and walks of life, especially my black and Latino brothers and sisters.

DJ Cool Clyde created United We Stand Entertainment (www.unitedwe-standent.org), a non-profit organization that explains the history of the Hip Hop Culture and where it originated, the South Bronx at Rosedale "Big" Park.

UWSE gives people, both young and mature, a platform to express their ideas, concerns and feelings on a one-on-one basis and in front of large crowds of people on television and radio, at parties, in newspapers and now in books.

I use hip hop music as a tool to draw our youth in and arm them with information, letting them know they can become Hip Hop professionals, such as Hip Hop Doctors, Hip Hop Lawyers, Hip Hop Accountants, Hip Hop Scientists, etc. and to give them information on health-related issues.

It's one thing to say you're going to do something, meaning lip service, and actually executing it, but Cool Clyde carries it out through the vibration, strength and blood of Christ.

I don't have hate for anyone but I hate the wrongs that they do.

I'd like to thank my cousin DJ Lightnin Lance, my sister MC Lil ShaRock, my Chief Administrative Officer, Shawn Webber, The Bronx Bullies and The Amen Rai of Hip Hop Afrika Bambaataa (Universal Zulu Nation).

Shout out to the Hypnotizing 3 MC's, my mother Beverly Hinds (R.I.P.) and the late, great Hip Hop Pioneer, Disco King Mario from the Black Spades Gang, and the Bronxdale Houses in the Bronx.

Bridges

The Reverend Kendra McIntosh
"Momma K"
Formerly Lilly Fellow, St. James Manhattan, New York

THE CITY OF NEW YORK is famous for its bridges: the Brooklyn Bridge; the George Washington Bridge; the "feeling groovy" 59th Street Bridge. Dozens of bridges connect places, people and neighborhoods with one another. The steel, cables, and concrete of these bridges facilitate unlikely partnerships; the Madison Avenue Bridge links the posh Upper Eastside and the gritty South Bronx.

The HipHopEMass worship service also serves as a bridge by bringing hip hop culture to Episcopal worship and uniting people from all walks of life in Christian worship and fellowship.

The HipHopEMass draws together the spirit-filled energy of hip hop culture and the time-tested, traditional worship of the Episcopal Church. HipHopEMass is the joining of street and altar in a new way, with a new rhythm. **The Spirit moves through the thumping pulse of the beat**, reviving tired prayers and timid worship, reaching out to both the children of the street and the elders of privilege. The service embodies full, dynamic community worship, pushing past quiet, individual, inward contemplation. Thus, celebration of the HipHopEMass expands into a corporate experience of the kingdom, where **we are all one.**

The ritual of the early church has been coupled with a new urban beat, merging orthodoxy and everyday life. **Together we say the 23rd Psalm** in the language of the streets and follow with the traditional version of the Lord's Prayer. The **"hood of death" meets "thy kingdom."** For me, this worship is the best example of the blessing of unity—it speaks to people of wealth and to those in great need, to the educated and of survivors, to people of color and to people of power. Looking out into the sea of faces, all swaying to the cadence of the music, one realizes that **there is no black or white, no male or female, no rich or poor, no young or old, no churched or unchurched, no South Bronx or Upper Eastside. We are all one in Christ.**

God's Mission Today–Hip Hop Mass

The Reverend Dr. James B. Lemler
Director of Mission
The Episcopal Church

IT WAS IN HIS HOMETOWN, in the synagogue where he grew up, and on the streets with which he was familiar that Jesus of Nazareth took the scroll of the prophet Isaiah and read these words: "The Spirit of the Lord is upon me, because he has anointed me to preach the Good News to the poor; he has sent me to heal the broken-hearted, to preach deliverance to the captives, and the recovering of sight to the blind, to set at liberty the oppressed. To proclaim the acceptable year of the Lord." Then Jesus rolled up the scroll and said, "Today, this day... this scripture is fulfilled in your hearing." (Luke 4:18-21)

That's how Jesus introduced his call and his mission. The actions of this mission were powerful and profound: preaching, providing hope for the poor, wholeness and healing for the broken, release and redemption for the captive, sight for the blind, liberty for the oppressed, and relaying the Good News of God's powerful work. This was Jesus' mission as it emerged in his birthplace, and in his own place of prayer. He lived that mission throughout his years of ministry, and it later became the mission of his followers.

God has inspired various revivals of that mission in a variety of ways and at different times throughout the past 2,000 years. Often those revivals have come from the streets, arising from the people, and through the power of song. HipHopEMass is a revival for our time. It came from the streets, from the people, and uses the power of song. Its themes are those of Christ's Gospel mission: good news, restoration, liberty, and new life. It is rooted in a context where God is at work and may be found.

The first time I experienced HipHopEMass was with hundreds of young people. It was clear that something important was happening. The experience connected so directly with the lives of the youth who were gathered and proclaimed the Gospel in a way that was relevant to their experience. There was a mood of celebration and anticipation.

The mission of the Church is restoration, invitation, and reconciliation. HipHopEMass presents this mission in a way that is rooted in the language of the people and that proclaims the Gospels' message with conviction and hope. This is so very important to human beings, and it is important to God's Church as well. The Church has been culturally captive in many ways for far too long. We have often opted for forms of worship and celebration that may have a traditional integrity but do not reflect the movement of the Spirit that has emerged in new ways and in new forms. HipHopEMass helps us to move into new realms of the Spirit and new expressions of the culture itself. It is a manifestation of the mission of God's people.

God's mission is for the whole world, because "God so loved the world..." HipHopEMass is a part of that global mission as well. It is a bridge of peace, hope, and reconciliation in a greatly fragmented world. The music, praise, and worship transcend cultural divides and present the gospel of reconciliation in a way that speaks to people everywhere. It is part of the vision of God's Reign and Rule which embraces the entire world. The recognition which HipHopEMass is receiving is an indication that spiritual seeking and searching is happening all over God's earth.

The first thing Jesus said when he identified his mission in the Nazarene synagogue was this: "The Spirit of the Lord has anointed me...." (Luke 4:18) That was about him, and it is about us as well. We are anointed by the Spirit of God for mission. HipHopEMass is a Spirit-filled anointing in and of itself. It makes a space for the Spirit to enter, to inspire, to fill, and to fulfill. HipHopEMass is part of the renewal and revival of the Spirit for our time and our place.

Amen... WORD!

The Music of EMass

Jeanine Otis
"Queen Jahneen"
Recording artist, singer and Rap Hall of Famer

THE MUSIC AND RHYTHM of the spoken word included in the EMass proclaims hope for the future. The word's existential foundation is built on tradition, which is the existence of a solid connection between the generations. The bridge is tradition: spiritual and African.

Cornell West states in his article, "Democracy Matters: The Necessary Engagement of Youth Culture": "Although Hip Hop Culture has become tainted by the very excesses and amorality it was born in rage against, the best of rap music...'prophetic rap'" as he has labeled it "....and Hip Hop Culture still expresses stronger and more clearly than any cultural expression in the past generation. Prophetic Hip Hop has told painful truths about the internal struggles and how the decrepit schools, inadequate healthcare, unemployment, and drug markets of the urban centers of the American empire have wounded their souls."

In African American tradition, "congregational singing is the means by which diverse individuals and groups worship the Savior as one committed union, and can provide expression for the deepest yearnings. Much of the congregational singing is executed in the responsorial (call and response) manner between a soloist and the congregation..." (as stated by Horace Boyer in the preface to Lift Every Voice and Sing II, Church Publishing Inc.).

The EMass music and rhythmical spoken word at its best is used creatively to explore the human condition, to express and expunge the doubt and uncertainty of being, and finally, to uplift and strengthen the spiritual community. From the opening Choral Introit, "God is in the House", which is repeated with a rhythmic response to indicate knocking, the beginning of the worship is reminiscent of the beginning of any number of ancient rituals from various cultures. Then, following the "knocking" is the prophetic answer found in the lyrics of "Jesus Walks," recorded by Kanye West, which sets the tone for hope: "Jesus walks...Jesus walks with me." This brings us back in its sentiment to: "I Want Jesus to Walk with Me. All along my pilgrim's journey..... I want Jesus to walk with me."

This worship experience enlists the three primary characteristics of African-American music—Call and Response, Syncopation/Rhythm and Improvisation—to bring new meaning to the traditional service order in *the*

Book of Common Prayer. For example, in the Liturgy of the Word, the prophetic, lyrical Remnant member, Niles, offers this thought as a refrain/mantra:

> If my people who were called by my name
> Would cut the conceit, bend their knees and just pray,
> And seek my face in this heavenly place
> I would listen, forgive them, and heal the land that they waste.

Hip hop culture has most assuredly co-opted the more traditional music of Rhythm and Blues/ Soul Music continually using the lyrical themes of that genre as refrains, or hooks. The Offertory and Communion of EMass incorporates both already recorded R&B/Soul and original music. A profound example of original Soul/Gospel/R&B can be found in the original music of Julio Herrera:

> We are redeemed of the Lord, so stand up and praise and magnify his holy name ....Let all of the Saints who believe in Jesus name lift up holy hands and show that he Reigns

We are redeemed, renewed, and charged to believe in our faith and our culture and to continue to engage ourselves to grow spiritually so that we can engage others.

HipHopEMass

Horace Clarence Boyer, PhD
Editor
Lift Every Voice and Sing II – An African American Hymnal

I WAS TOTALLY UNPREPARED to like—or even understand—the HipHopEMass. To be absolutely honest, I attended the service that Tuesday night, November 15, 2005, at the beautiful chapel at North Carolina's Kanuga Conference Center more out of a feeling of obligation, and perhaps a modicum of curiosity, than a desire to worship in one of the many and varied styles with which the Lord has blessed us. I actually attended as music director of the conference, during which the mass was to be celebrated.

Since I was unprepared to like the mass I was (more than) a little chagrined at not having the proper emotions to reconcile my complete **involvement** in this highly unusual but extremely spiritual celebration. **The sonorous and rhythmic phrases of the rappers and the tunes and harmonies of the singers brought a meaning and passion to the scripture, prayers and responses that must have been what Christ had in mind when he taught his prayer that begins "Our Father..."**

To be sure, the HipHopEMass does not contain the familiar phrases and cadences of the 1928 Prayer Book nor Hymnal 1940, nor does it overflow with the well-known sentences of the 1979 Prayer Book nor the friendly songs of Hymnal 1982. What it does contain, however, is the **powerful** and **urgent** language and rhythm of today's speech and the evocative sincerity and infectious beat of today's music. **And most importantly, it contains the innocence and honesty of the young!**

As I left the mass that November evening I realized that I had just witnessed the church of the future!

Word!

Glossary

WORD	DEFINITION
anoint	to bless with oil
back-up	from the police term: having reinforcement; having the support of one's friends who will "cover your back"
baller	ballplayer, someone who is good at playing basketball and has become successful at it, earning a lot of money and attention
ballin'	to have it all
blast	to "put someone on blast": to call them out as being wrong
bling or bling, bling	material wealth; or the possession of material wealth; jewelry, derived from the sound made in cartoons by light shining off of a diamond
cats	men, enemies
chill	to relax, something that is relaxed and cool
chillin'	relaxing, taking it easy
chill out	to relax and take it easy
crew	one's group, band, friends
crib	one's home
def	Excellent, derived from definite and death
dis or diss	to insult, short for dismiss
dog	best friend, good friend, partner
down low	covert, secret, "hush hush," derived from low profile
enuff	enough
fa sho	for sure
fam	family
floss	to show off
fly	attractive, beautiful
game	in the game, whatever the game might be. A game is some way to make money or advance oneself, or is literally, a game

hater	one who despises or speaks ill of another
have your back	to support a friend; to "cover your back"
heated	emotionally charged
holla back	to contact someone, to call back
Holy Communion	The Lord's Supper, the Eucharist, the Mass, the Great Offering. This is the sacrament that Christ commanded his followers to celebrate as a means to remember his life, death, and resurrection, until his second coming
homies	good friends, friends or acquaintances
hood	the 'hood, derived from neighborhood
hoodie	a t-shirt or sweatshirt with a hood attached to it
hook	a verse or line in a song that makes it easy to like or remember
keeping it real	being true to oneself, not putting on airs
kicks	shoes
MC	Jamaican in origin as a hip hop term, an acronym for "Master of Ceremonies." The MC was the only person at a gathering who was allowed to use the microphone. Can also stand for Microphone Controller and Mic Checka (checker); Emcee, a skilled rapper
mic	short for microphone, pronounced "mike"
paper	money
peeps	one's people or friends
player	one who is "true to the hood"
player-haters	one who despises or speaks ill of another player because he does not have any game of his own.
pose	to pretend to be something you're not, to be an imposter
posse	a group of people one "hangs out with," not necessarily a gang
props	an abbreviation of "propers" or proper respects. At an award ceremony, the winner gives props: "And I would like to thank..."
reconciliation	the sacrament of penance whereby sins are absolved through confession and forgiveness
represent	to stand for something one is convinced of and feels related to, and to express that feeling. For example: to represent one's family, upbringing, neighborhood, values

shout out	giving one's respect through a mention in a rap, graffiti, or other means of expression
South Bronx	an area of one of the five boroughs (or districts) of the city of New York; the birthplace of hip hop
step to	to engage in a confrontation; opposite of "step off"
The Book of Common Prayer	the official book giving the order and content of services in the Episcopal Church
The Southern Christian Leadership Conference	(SCLC) the organization of black churches and ministers which, under the leadership of Martin Luther King, Jr., formed the backbone of the civil rights movement in the US during the 1950s and 1960s
tight	a state of mind; feeling really good at the moment; straight, legitimate, all-good
twisted	to get it wrong
wit	with
word	1) (n.) Biblical (John 1:1). "logos": truth 2) (interj.) exclamation or term of endearment
yo	1) (n.) you 2) (adj.) your 3) (interj.) to catch attention, as in "Yo! What's up?"

TIMELINE $\boxed{\text{FINAL}}$ + G-O-D Is in the House!

EYE Hip Hop Celebration *Inspired by HipHopEMass.org*
The Episcopal Youth Event + Berea, Kentucky
Vigil of Mary and Martha of Bethany + Thursday, July 28, 2005 + 8:30 p.m. CDST
Rehearsal Thursday, July 28, 2:00-4:00 p.m. & 7:00 p.m.

✠ ✠ ✠

The Holy Eucharist
Order of Hip ✠ Yes, Yes Ya'll! ✠ God Loves You!

8:30 p.m.	Welcome	EYE Leadership Posse – Sandra, RC & Poppa T
	Warm-Up	Queen Jahneen & MC D.O.
		Greetings & intros from EYE & HipHopEMass.org SBXNYC
		Tradition of Call & Response – *Amen! Word!*
		Hip Hop Soliloquy + *Challenge to the Church!* by The Remnant!
8:35 p.m.		Processional Hip + *God Is In The House!* into *Jesus Walks* (West)
		Led by Jahneen, D.O., D. Cross, The Remnant, EYE Music Team & Choir, Dancers, Color Bearers & All Rappers of God!
8:47 p.m.		Opening Acclamation, Celebrant + Backbeat *TupacBiggie*
8:50 p.m.		Hip Psalmody 33:1-11, Rap by Huitzin + Backbeat *Huitzin*
8:55 p.m.		Gospel Hip + Rap on OBP ("Off the Beaten Path"/Luke 10:38-42 ("Mary and Martha") D., D.O. & loop
9:02 p.m.	THE WORD	The Holy Gospel + Luke 10:38-42 by The Revd. Katherine Tate, Gospeller + Backbeat Zion
9:05 p.m.		The Homily + The Testifiers with D.O. on mic + Backbeat *Zion*
9:15 p.m.	ALTAR CALL	Prayers (Freestyle), Confession, Absolution & The Peace
	HOLY ANOINTING	Led by Clergy, Rappers and All the People of God + Backbeat *TupacBiggie*
9:25 p.m. OBP Hip		Offertory Hip + The Remnant with Queen Jahneen, D. Cross & Hop Choir & Dancers
		Offering for hip hop ministry in prisons and at-risk youth facilities across USA?
9:30 p.m.	HOLY EUCHARIST	The Greatest, Biggest and Most Awesome Up + Backbeat *Be Thou My Vision* DOWNBEAT ✠ The Lord's Prayer & Holy Communion + *Be Thou My Vision* INTO UPBEAT with *Alleluia!* Jahneen, Choir & Rap. Also, 1) Lean on Me and 2) Hail Jesus!
9:55 p.m.	ST. MIKE TIME	Post-Communion Prayer & Hip + D. & D.O. with The Remnant & All the People of God!
9:59 p.m.		The Pontifical Hip Hop Blessing + Big Poppa V!
10:00 p.m.		Recession Hip + *Jesus Walks*
		Led By All the Children of God!
10:10 p.m.		And That Ain't All Ya'll! To Late Night!

HipHopEMass.org DJ MASS

"Dear Momma + One More Chance"
TupacBiggie 2004-05

THE HOLY EUCHARIST *Let's Show God Some Love!*
THE BOOK OF COMMON PRAYER (Episcopal)
An Order for Celebrating the Holy Eucharist (400)

DJ MASS + MASTER MIX
Written, Compiled, Adapted and Arranged by
Kurtis Blow, DJ Cool Clyde, Derrell Edwards, Julio Herrera, Timothy Holder,
DJ Lightnin' Lance, Tom Mercer, DJ Ol' School Sam & Shake, Jahneen Otis,
Martha Overall, Catherine Roskam & All the People of **HipHopEMass.org**!

✠ ✠ ✠

	ORDER OF HIP	**RITE** *TupacBiggie*
Minutes -20-0	Prelude Hip	
	Backbeat	Tupac/Biggie
	Loops	Kurtis Blow
	Welcome by MC / Celebrant	
	"Amen! WORD!"	With loop
	I Can't Believe	
	....	
Minutes 1-5	Procession Hip	
	Jesus Walks	Kanye West
Minute 6	Opening Acclamation and Prayer	
	Backbeat	Tupac/Biggie
Minutes 7-10	A Def Reading	Continues
Minutes 10-15	The Psalm *Rap*	Continues UPBEAT
Minutes 15-20 THE WORD	Gospel Hip	
	The Time Has Come	Corey Red and Precise
Minutes 20-25	The Holy Gospel	
	Backbeat	Koltai
Minutes 25-35	The Sermon	
	Backbeat	Tupac/Biggie
Minutes 35-40 ALTAR CALL & HOLY ANOINTING	Altar Call with Prayers, Anointing & Confession	
	Backbeat	Tupac/Biggie
Minutes 40-45	Offertory Hip	
	One Way	BBJ
Minutes 45-55 HOLY EUCHARIST	The Holy Eucharist	
	Backbeat	Tupac/Biggie
	The Lord's Prayer and Holy Communion	
	Alleluia, Unity Klan	
	Holy Culture, Crossroad	
Minutes 55-57	Post Communion Prayer	
	Backbeat	Tupac/Biggie
Minutes 57-60	Dance Recessional	
	Jesus Walks	Kanye West
	....	
Minutes +60-80	Postlude + *Dance* Hip	
	I Know I Can	Nas
	We've Got Love	Third World

Discography

New to hip hop? Here's some of the music the HipHopEMass has used to good effect in different parts of a typical service. Many of the songs are from the HipHopEMass' album, *And the Word was Hip Hop*, which is designed to match up with the events of a service.

(None of the songs listed contain objectionable language, though some are found on albums where explicit lyrics appear on other tracks.)

Processional

Jesus Walks
Kanye West on the album *The College Dropout*

Work That
Mary J. Blige on the album *Growing Pains*

One Mic, One Love
D.O. on the album *And the Word Was Hip Hop*

Gospel

Heaven
The Missionary Men on the album *And the Word Was Hip Hop*

Signs
D.O. on the album *And the Word Was Hip Hop*

Offertory

I Can
Nas on the album *God's Son*

Grace, Hope, and Faith
D. Cross on the album *And the Word Was Hip Hop*

Unbelievable
The Remnant on the album *And the Word Was Hip Hop*

Communion

God is Love
D.O. on the album *And the Word Was Hip Hop*

Happiness
Missionary Men on the album *And the Word Was Hip Hop*

Recessional

Keep Ya Head Up
Tupac Shakur on the album *Greatest Hits*

I am Hip Hop
D. Cross on the album *And the Word Was Hip Hop*

RESPECT, SHOUTS OUT! & Big Ups

ACKNOWLEDGEMENTS *From* **Poppa T** *Editor-in-Chief*

✠ ✠ ✠

Poet, Prophet **Tupac Shakur** 1971-1996
Champion of the 'Roses That Grow from Concrete'

María Guadalupe *Madre de las Americas* + **Black Madonna**
Where the Poor Are Served There Roses Bloom in December

For All the People & All the Gifts of God*HipHop*
GIVE THANKS!

The Trinity Hip Hop Mass ✠ *Fridays, June 11-July 23, 2004*
HipHopEMass ✠ *Founded October 3, 2004*

St. Mark's in-the-Bowery Episcopal Church and Free Choir
First Hip Hop Celebrations Advent 2004 on the Lower East Side NYC
Joined Trinity Hip Hop Mass, July 2, 2004

𝔉 𝔬 𝔱

All the Children of Trinity Episcopal Church of Morrisania, the South Bronx USA, the Diocese of New York, the Episcopal Church, the Nation and the World ✠ *You Lead the Way! (Mark 10:13-16)*

All of the MCs, DJs, Rappers, Singers & Voices, Dancers & Artists of HipHopEMass ✠ *Amen!* (& Named That by His Grandmother); Bernadette Cleare; *Big Tone & Kool-D*; Kurtis Blow *The King of Rap* & All the Rappers of Hip Hop Church, Harlem and L.A.; Cool Clyde & Lightnin Lance *1st to Scratch Wax Worldwide* & HIP HOP ICONS and All the People of *United We Stand, Rosedale Park Kings and Queens Summer Festival 2004-05*; D. Cross *Living Instrument, Beatbox Extraordinaire; Crystal Agape* Page; D.O. *(Defy the Odds) True Freestyle King;* Derek *Math Man; ELIJAH Boy* Wonder! Get Gospel and *Get It Good* with Paradox, Tamara, The Missionary Men - Mr. Monk and Jahdiel *with* Chris *Rock* Belmont and *Syntax; Glory* Dominique Singletary, Vic Howell and Rayniel Delvalle *HipHopCrooner;* Tripp Levine *Gumbo Jumbo;* Lamar Haney *Noah,* Donavan Bratton *& SHADES OF FAITH; Manifestation of Praise;* Jeannine Otis *JAHNEEN, ALL RISE FOR THE QUEEN!* Kelvin *GOLDENLORD* Lopez; Kenny Williams; Jessye Nicole Smith + *The Mighty, Mighty Remnant – Genesis* Adam Beane, *Diatribes* Niles Gray & *Just John* John Jordan; Alex *S.E.V.E.N.* Spearman; *Sweet P* Michelle Perkins; & Desean Wilson SBX+USA!

THE RAPPERS Are THE MESSENGERS OF GOD!

The HipHopEMass Band: *Let the Remix and the Rebirth Begin!*
Soul Man Julio Herrera *Music Director, Keyboards & Vocals*
Wizard David Koltai *Lead Guitar* + *Godfather* David Burnett *Bass Guitar*
Beat I Keith Watts *Drums* + *Beat II* Michael Flythe *Drums*

In Thanksgiving for the Fathers and Mothers of Hip Hop Culture Who Bless HipHopEMass

Afrika Bambaata *Father of Hip Hop Culture*; Kurtis Blow *The King of Rap* My Teacher and Mentor; Cool Clyde and Lightnin Lance *First to Scratch Wax Worldwide* who had an Episcopal Priest bless 3,000 at Rosedale Park from the Gospel of Jesus Christ*HipHop*; *Godfather* David Burnett *The Faithful*; Jeannine Otis "Jahneen" *Rap Hall of Fame, Sister and Spiritual Light, Truly Queen of HipHopEMass* & Blessings Phat upon All the Founders of Hip Hop *Old School, New School & Schools To Come!*

Beloved Editors and Messengers of *The Hip Hop Prayer Book* and cd, *And The Word Was Hip Hop*

D. Cross *Glory & Shine;* D.O. *Word Master;* Peter Grandell (The Revd.) *Faith & Service;* John Jordan *Preacher-Man;* Kendra McIntosh (The Revd.) *Rock;* Jeannine Otis *Spirit, Grace & Love;* Jennifer Phillips (The Revd.) *New Promise* + Julio Herrera, Producer, And the Word Was Hip Hop *Remix & Rebirth*

& Esteemed Messengers of The Foreward & AfterWORD

Michael Curry (The Rt. Revd.), The Bishop of North Carolina; Catherine Roskam (The Rt. Revd.), The Bishop Suffragan of New York; Lynne Washington (The Revd.), The Diocese of Virginia; Peter Grandell (The Revd.), The Diocese of Pennsylvania; Eric Hinds *Cool Clyde*, Bronx, New York; James Lemler (The Revd. Dr.), Episcopal Church USA; Kendra McIntosh (The Revd.), The Diocese of New York; Horace Boyer (Dr.), *General Editor, Lift Every Voice & Sing* + *Our King of Gospel* & Jeannine Otis, The Diocese of New York

All Priests, Pastors, Friends and Contributors ✠ Founders of The Trinity Hip Hop Mass

Spring & Summer 2004 + *Especially* Lyndon Harris (The Revd.) *Cathedral of Saint John the Divine NYC*; Barbara Kearse (The Revd.) and her nephew, Ryan *Transfiguration Lutheran Church, Harlem – Thank You for the 23rd Psalm*; Tom Mercer (The Revd.) and the children and young people of *St. Paul's Episcopal Church, Bronx –Thank You for the Confession, the Awesome Sanctus, the Words of Institution and*, Lamont Dean, *a Bronx teenager, for The "Pontifical Hip Hop Blessing" first given by* Donald Taylor (The Vicar Bishop of the City of New York) *the First Trinity Hip Hop Mass, June 11, 2004!* Also, Martha Overall (The

Revd.) *St. Ann's Episcopal Chruch, Bronx – Thank You for giving us your experience, spirit and love and for Celebrating our first prison mass at Beaumont, Virginia, August 24, 2004; DJ's* Ol School Sam and Shake; SCRIBE *Deluxe* Becky Garrison – *WOW!* Derrell Edwards, *'Producer,' 1st Master Mix/Playlist; Trinity Seminarians* Noah Evans (2003-04) and Matthew Stewart *both honoring The General Theological Seminary and The Episcopal Diocese of Massachusetts*; Erin Shanks *Hip Hop Vacation Church School* + Summer 2004 Intern *Smith College, The Episcopal Diocese of Alabama*; Julio Calderon *Artist and Set Design*; Gene Hoist, Malcolm Emmanuel, Jose Rodriguez and The Working Crew *Trinity Episcopal Church of Morrisania, Altar Guild and Hard Workers All! & To All the Children and Young People Who Danced the Night Away & To All Who Looked On Celebrating from High Above in "Cathedral Towers" of the Street, Project High Rises of the Hood!* For all the priestly celebrants and supporters, Howard Blunt (The Revd.), Hilario Albert (The Revd.), Bert Bennett (The Revd.), Silvia Vasquez (The Revd. Canon), Michael Kendall (The Ven.), Steve Shanks (the Revd.), Sarah Irwin (The Revd.), Diego Delgado (The Revd.); Ann DuBose Hare (The Revd.) & Douglas Fisher (The Revd.); Andrea R. Hayden (The Revd.) & Archdeacon Tai Tuatagagaloa-Matalavea, Anglican Observer at the United Nations

All Thanks & Love to the People of Trinity Episcopal Church of Morrisania, Bronx, New York *HipHop* **& Not! God Loves Us All!** Lillas Bogle, Senior Warden; Keith Warren, Junior Warden; JoAnn Lake, Secretary; and, Marjorie Jones, Treasurer + Eileen Emmanuel, Office Secretary; Sam Cannon, Sexton; Rodger Emmanuel, Mark Cyr (The Revd.) Web Managers *HipHopEMass.org*; Ruth Gardner *First Hip Hop Vestments in beautiful royal kinte*; Gene Hoist *Altar Guild*; Florence Anthony *Usher & Trainer of Ushers*; All the Supporters and Workers for *Every Friday Night & Children's Sunday Morning Breakfast* especially Carol Baird, Sonia Bird, Jackie Carlos, Shelly Jenkins, Chavone Lake, Elvin Maxwell + *Rest in Peace*, Leona and Ira Ross, Jeanie Seaman, Sacha Thomas, Phil Tomlinson; To Those Faithful Who Walked the Neighborhood Inviting People to the Celebration! To All Who gave time, talent, treasure and Prayer! *To those who supported our children and young people in any way! To God be The Glory!*

LOVE YOU BIG 1st Friday POSSE! Kaileen Alston *& Newark*; Kurt Dunkle (The Revd.) & Diocese of Florida; Patrick Kidd, Peggy Pook & St. James Manhattan; Alison Lutz, Gerry Becker & Stuart Hoke (The Revd.)& Trinity + St. Paul's NYC; Billy Wormell & All the Young People of Grace Millbrook, Hip Hop Ushers

May We Never Forget Hip Hop Santa The Hon. Kenny Agosto *Bronx Democratic Party*

The Hon. Reuben Diaz, Jr., *Assemblyman from Hip Hop* **SBX ✠ USA** Made it real, *I AM HIP HOP!* The Hon. Michael and Kennedy Benjamin, New York State Assembly, **SBX ✠ USA**

The Thousands and Thousands More Who Are Celebrating *GodHipHopEverywhere!*

The Trinity Hip Hop Street Masses *Fridays* June 11-July 23, 2004 + Trinity Avenue at 166th SBX+USA HipHopEMass *Sundays* October 3-31 *with* Kurtis Blow, the King of Rap, *Bishop Roskam & Bishop Tengatenga, Southern Malawi, KICKIN OFF!* Trinity Episcopal Church of Morrisania, Bronx, New York + *Our Home 1st Fridays* + December 3, 2004- + *Momma K, Poppa Ibe & More!*

YES! YES! Y'ALL!

Rosedale Park Hip Hop Celebration *with Cool Clyde and Founders* + *MAKIN BRONX Kings and Queens* + Sunday, August 8, 2004. Beaumont, Virginia, Correctional Facility, August 24, 2004 + Barbara Marques, Chaplain and Marjorie Holm, Chaplain *Deerfield Prison*. United States Conference, World Council of Churches, Atlanta + October 5, 2004 *Blessed Are the Peacemakers.*

Episcopal Social Services *Bronx Homes Homecoming Celebration* + Thursday, October 21, 2004. 228th Convention of Diocese of NY, Tarrytown, November 12, 2004 + *600 stood to rap the 23rd Psalm! LOVE YOU EPISCOPALIANS!* Cathedral of Saint John the Divine, New York, December 4, 2004 + Celebrating Diocese of New York YOUTH RALLY. Harlem Women's Shelter's *Hip Hop Blessing* + December 16, 2004.

Southern Christian Leadership Conference, Hampton, Virginia + January 29, 2005 *Dr. Martin Luther King, Jr. Leadership Award*. Memphis Theological Seminary + April 26, 2005 + *Memphis Soultown WELCOMES HipHopEMass! LET SHOW GOD SOME LOVE!* Province II, The Episcopal Church, Albany, New York + May 13, 2005 *THE RAPPERS ARE THE MESSENGERS.* EPIS-CO-BUILD Street Mass Newburgh, New York + *God Bless You Episcopal Churches & Friends of HIP HOP HABITAT!* 1,400 Teenagers & 55 Bishops OFF THE BEATEN PATH at Episcopal Youth Event + Berea, Kentucky July 28, 2005. *August 14, 2005* + UNITED WE STAND *Rosedale Park, Bronx NY CELEBRATIONS* with Cool Clyde and Founders. *Beautiful* HipHopEMass, *Beautiful* Staten Island, Sunday evening, September 18, 2005 + *Hip Hop Givin Us the Rhythm of Life.* Another HipHopEMass STREET CELEBRA-TION + WE LOVE YOU St. Paul's Poughkeepsie, September 24, 2005.

TRANSFORMATION & RENEWAL IV, Kanuga, North Carolina, November 15, 2005 + HIP HOP MOUNTAIN-TOP. **Two parishes in Virginia and one in Kentucky begin HipHopEMass Celebrations + December 2005 and January 2006**

Bishop Councill *Big Poppa G of New JerSEY leads* 300 Teenagers at Trinity Cathedral *HipHopEMass* + January 27, 2006. *GOD BLESS TEXAS!* Absalom Jones Celebration at St. Martin's with Bishops Don Wimberly and Hebert Thompson. And then on over to ST. LUKE'S Sunday Mornin *HipHopEMass*, TEXAS SOUTHERN UNIVERSITY + February 18-19, 2006 *& GOD BLESS NEWARK*! Saturday, March 25, 2006: Celebrations and Workshops for Youth and Adults at St. Paul's Paterson NJ. *SNAP IT OUT IN MISSISSIPPI!* Hip Hop Nite Prayers at Piney Woods School + April 6, 2006 *SUPREME! GOD DID IT!* JOINT SERVICE with Hip Hop Church Harlem + *Celebrating Kurtis Blow's 1st Sermon* + GreaterHood AME Church + April 6, 2006

AND THAT AIN'T ALL Y'ALL!

The World Council of Churches, Southern Christan Leadership Conference, & Harvard Divinity School who have beautifully honored the work and mission of HipHopEMass

All donors and benefactors $ who have made it possible for HipHopEMass to SHINE!

Thank You to an anonymous donor who contributed seed money at the beginning; to Scot McComas (The Revd.) of Charlotte, North Carolina who gave and raised transition monies to create "HipHopEMass" from summer to fall 2004; and, to Audrey Gonzalez (The Revd.) of Memphis, Tennessee who under-wrote masses into 2006. To **All** who have given, our love and thanks. **We also thank** Trinity Grants of Trinity Wall Street + St. Paul's for their generous gift for board development and mission planning as we grow, God Willing, into a full-time congregation and parish of the Episcopal Church. **To Bishops and Dioceses near and far** who know mission when they see it. Thank you and bless you for your generosity and faith. **We love you** Office of Black Ministries and Union of Black Episcopalians for your prayers, support and leadership. And to Youth Organizations Everywhere, *LEAD ON!*

Mission Graphics, Church of Our Savior, Chinatown NYC + *25,000 Mass Cards and More!* We love you Peter, Jimmy and Charlie Chan *1st Hip Hop Blessing in Chinese, November 5, 2004*

✠ ✠ ✠

The partnership, friendship, faith and support **Break of Dawn** of Church Publishing, Incorporated meant **Beautiful Sunshine** in the First Years of this Amazing Ministry. We thank God for Ken Arnold, Publisher, Hero and Hip Hop Deacon & for Lucas Smith, who guided and dreamed when few others could or knew how to, more than hip hop editor

HipHopEMass Heart! For ever and ever!
cuz Hip Hop Don't Stop!

And we gotta throw some Big Ups to CPI Peeps, Frank Tedeschi, Liturgical Editor and Sage & Mark Dazzo, Marketing Director *Patience of Job/Vision of Isiah. Thank You* Joan Castagnone and Johnny Ross for visiting *Hip Hop Jerusalem* August 2004!

A Great Missionary Bishop, Bill Stough of Alabama *d. 2004* taught me well *The Best Mission Begins at Home!* **LONG LIVE STREET & ALTAR**

And to my three Bishops, the Great Bishops of the Great Diocese of New York MY GRATITUDE & LOVE. The Rt. Revds. Mark Sisk *Diocesan*, Catherine Roskam *Suffragan* & Donald Taylor *Vicar Bishop, City of New York.*

And to my homies FOR REAL, who love me. I love you

Jamie, Brad, Jennifer, Scot, All the Rappers, KD, Julio & Jeannine, Jane, Mom & Dad!

"Poppa T!"
Timothy Holder (The Revd.)

✠ ✠ ✠

***Supreme!* GOD DID IT!**

If Jesus were alive today,
He would have been a Rapper.

—THE RT. REV. CATHERINE S ROSKAM
Founding Bishop, HipHopEMass

Enjoy The Hip Hop Prayer Book?

Try these:

....

And the Word Was Hip Hop

An original full-length album from the creators of *The Hip Hop Prayer Book.*

....

The Gathering
City Prayers, City Hopes

A powerful collection of prayers and reflections from rappers, both known and unknown, and inner city and incarcerated youth. A moving, unconventional, expression of spirituality.

....

Disciples of the Street
The Promise of a Hip Hop Church

The story of the HipHopEMass, and the definitive look at how religion and hip hop interact.

"This is a stunner. Eric Gutierrez opens closed windows of the soul and delivers an utterly challenging, refreshingly original work. Read it."

—Malcolm Boyd, Author of *Are You Running with me, Jesus?*